DIVE INTO HISTORY

VOLUM

U.S.

SUBMARINES

HENRY C. KEATTS and GEORGE C. FARR

Pisces Books
A division of Gulf Publishing Company
Houston, Texas

To Carole and Nancy,
two lovely and very patient ladies

VOLUME 2:
U.S.
SUBMARINES

DIVE INTO HISTORY is a trademark of Pisces Books/
Gulf Publishing Company.

Library of Congress Cataloging-in-Publication Data
Keatts, Henry.
  U.S. submarines / Henry C. Keatts and George C. Farr.
  p.   cm. — (Dive into history ; v. 2)
  Includes index.
  ISBN 1-55992-047-5
  1. United States—History, Naval.   2. Submarine boats—Atlantic
Coast (U.S.)—History.   3. Shipwrecks—Atlantic Coast (U.S.)—
History.   4. Scuba diving—Atlantic Coast (U.S.)   I. Farr,
George.   II. Title.   III. Title: US submarines.   IV. Series: Dive into
history (Houston, Tex.) ; v. 2.
E182.K26   1991
359.3′2572′0973—dc20
                                                        91-7196
                                                         CIP
10 9 8 7 6 5 4 3 2 1

Printed in Hong Kong

CONTENTS

PREFACE

Submarine warfare dates from the use of diving bells by Alexander the Great in 332 B.C. at the siege of Tyre, but the bells' lack of propulsion made them more underwater enclosures than submarines. From the time of Leonardo da Vinci, men sketched plans for underwater vessels. In 1578, William Bourne, an Englishman, published the plans of a submarine in his *Inventions and Devises*. The plans indicated that surface and underwater propulsion was to be accomplished by rowing, but no working model was ever built. A Dutch chemist, Cornelius Van Drebbel (1572-1633), in the 17th century built the first self-propelled submarine. His wooden vessel had iron frames that were covered with greased leather. Water was taken into the hull for diving and expelled for surfacing by leather bulkheads that were screw-operated. Twelve oarsmen propelled the craft, whether above or under water. England's King James I witnessed a successful demonstration of the boat when Van Drebbel submerged it 15 feet beneath the Thames River, then resurfaced. The inventor had developed a system of maintaining pure air in his submarine, but the secret died with him in 1633.

A variety of other developments followed, including large stones that were fastened to the hull as ballast, then detached to surface, one time only. Another was the sealing of a 50-foot sloop for underwater use by an Englishman, John Day. He became the first recorded submarine fatality in 1774, when the sloop's hull collapsed at a depth of 130 feet.

The submarine reached its present state of the art in slow, painful, and often tragic stages. As described in this book's Introduction, that was particularly true in the United States.

Wreck diving has fostered archaeological and historical marine research. It has also collected rare artifacts from vessels that have rested at the bottom of the sea for decades, even centuries. The recovery, identification, dating, and preservation of those historical objects attract both amateur and professional archaeologists. Preservation is the moral responsibility of any diver who removes a relic from a sunken ship. The techniques of restoration and preservation of underwater artifacts are complicated, time-consuming, and costly.

A word to the wise: the passage of Congressional Bill HR74, the abandoned shipwreck bill, has given individual states the sovereignty to determine and interpret the status of all shipwrecks submerged in state waters. Divers should watch for ongoing developments resulting in increased clarification of this legislation.

Henry C. Keatts
George C. Farr

vi

ACKNOWLEDGMENTS

Without the contributions and cooperation of the following individuals and organizations, this book would not have been possible:

Frank Benoit	Chris Dillon	Bill Palmer
Steve Bielenda	Gary Gentile	Tom Roach
Bill Campbell	Don Gunning	Dave Robinson
Bill Carter	Aaron Hirsch	Stewart Robinson
James L. Christley	Jon Hulburt	Brad Sheard
Chip Cooper	Uwe Lovas	Brian Skerry
Billy Deans	Mike Moore	Ed Suarez
Michael DeCamp	Steve Moy	

American Underwater Search and Survey, Ltd.
National Archives
Naval Historical Center
Portsmouth (N.H.) Naval Shipyard
Submarine Force Library and Museum

And special thanks to Viking Diving Division for the use of their excellent diving suits and Poseidon regulators.

Locations of Wrecks

U.S. Submarine Development

The U.S. Navy's submarine force dates from the commissioning of U.S.S. *Holland* (SS-*1*) in 1900. However, the first United States contribution to submarine development was made during the American Revolution by David Bushnell, an undergraduate Yale student. He introduced screw propulsion, ballast tanks, and underwater offensive armament that resembled a mine more than a torpedo. Bushnell's vessel proved to be the first truly successful submarine. A one-man screw propelled the craft by manually operating two screw-propellers in the bow, one for horizontal propulsion and the other for vertical depth control.

Tanks in the bottom of the boat were flooded to submerge, using two hand pumps to expel the water ballast. Nine hundred pounds of lead ballast was attached outside the hull, 200 pounds of the lead could be dropped for emergency surfacing. Intake and exhaust ventilators provided surface ventilation; water pressure closed them while the vessel was submerged. A water gauge or barometer provided depth readings, and navigational guidance depended on a compass, with phosphorescent fungi added for visibility in darkness.

Bushnell completed his boat late in 1775, with help from his brother Ezra. He named it *Turtle* because the "barrel-stave" submarine looked like two upper tortoise shells of equal size, joined together. Tar was applied to the exterior for water-proofing. A small conning tower with glass ports, three sealable air vents, and a brass hatch were on top. A timber across the interior protected the sides from collapsing and provided a seat for the single crew member. The vessel could remain submerged for up to 30 minutes, and under ideal conditions, her top speed was 3 knots. She was armed only with an oak casing filled with 150 pounds of explosive. The casing was carried astern for attachment to the bottom of an enemy ship, then detonated by a clockwork mechanism. A wood screw auger, protruding from the top of the submarine could be turned into the hull of an intended victim, and left there. The barrel of explosive was attached to the

A cutaway model of the submarine Turtle, *designed and built by David Bushnell during the American Revolution. After the war, George Washington stated, "I then thought and still think the* Turtle *was an effort of genius."* (Photo by H. Keatts.)

wood screw by a line. Bushnell anchored a borrowed sloop in Long Island Sound as a target for his brother Ezra, who successfully attached several explosive charges to it from the submerged *Turtle*.

American Revolution

The military potential of the new boat as an offensive weapon against the British was clearly established. But Ezra became ill before it could be put into action. The search for a replacement produced another Ezra, Sergeant Ezra Lee, a volunteer from the Connecticut Militia. Manned by Sergeant Lee, *Turtle* earned distinction as the first submarine in history to attack an enemy ship.

On September 6, 1776 *Turtle* was moved to New York Harbor for her role in the American Revolution. Her entry was less than heroic as two rowboats towed her to within a few miles of the formidable British fleet. Lee chose his target—Admiral Richard Howe's impressive flagship, H.M.S. *Eagle*, a 64-gun ship-of-the-line. A strong tide carried the submarine past the warships, but Lee waited, with *Turtle*'s brass conning tower just awash, until the tide slackened. Then he maneuvered the submerged submarine under *Eagle* to attach the explosive charge. All went well until the attaching screw would not penetrate; it had hit an iron crossbar just forward of the rudder. Lee attempted to maneuver to another position under the warship, but as he later stated, the submarine slid out from under the enemy's hull and shot to the surface "with great velocity." Lee submerged *Turtle* again, but decided that "the best generalship" was to clear the area before the fast approaching dawn.

After the aborted action, many historians have claimed that Lee and *Turtle* failed to accomplish their mission because of the thick copper sheathing of *Eagle*'s hull. Many British warships were furnished with that protection against the ravages of the teredo (shipworms). *Eagle*, however, was not coppered until 1782, six years after the aborted attempt. Sergeant Lee barely escaped a British party rowing to one of the anchored warships. A chase ensued, during which Lee released his explosive device, which exploded violently. When the British seamen reported the American attempt, the Royal Navy warships were moved out of the harbor. Two other unsuccessful attacks were made in 1776, one by Lee, another by an operator whose name is believed to be Pratt. Bushnell finally gave up, stating, "I was unable to support myself, and the persons I must have employed, had I proceeded. Besides, I found it absolutely necessary, that the operators should acquire more skill in the management of the vessel, before I could expect success." No record of *Turtle*'s fate has been found. After the war, George Washington eulogized the early submarine and her inventor, "I then thought and still think the *Turtle* was an effort of genius."

The one-man submarine Turtle *made an unsuccessful attack in 1776 on Lord Admiral Richard Howe's flagship* Eagle *in New York Harbor. An exhausted Sergeant Ezra Lee holds onto the British warship's rudder after attempting to attach an explosive charge to her hull.* (Illustration courtesy of the Submarine Force Library and Museum.)

The next important contribution to submarine development is credited to another American, Robert Fulton, more widely acclaimed for his commercial success with the steamship *Clermont*. Fulton built the four-man submarine *Nautilus* in France, with financial support from the French government. She was 21 feet 4 inches long with a 6-foot 4-inch beam. Her noteworthy features were separate means of propulsion for surface and submerged cruising, horizontal hydroplanes for depth control, surface-floated hose for underwater air supply, anchor gear release from the interior and a copper hull over iron framework.

Sails provided surface propulsion; the mast was hinged and stowed in a deck groove while the boat was submerged; a hand-driven screw propelled the submarine underwater, and a rudder provided maneuverability. A hollow keel served as a ballast tank, taking in water to submerge and pumping it out to resurface. The detachable keel could be dropped for rapid surfacing in an emergency. A four-man crew could remain submerged for one hour. Fulton submerged *Nautilus* to a depth of 25 feet on July 9, 1800, and remained down for 17 minutes. Submerged runs at Paris, Brest, and Le Havre demonstrated that the submarine could be navigated successfully underwater.

Fulton added several offensive weapons that carried 80 to 100 pounds of gunpowder. They were not torpedoes, but they served the same purpose in a uniquely different manner. Unlike the self-propelled torpedoes of today's navies, Fulton's were towed under a target vessel, like underwater kites. When the explosives reached the hull of the intended victim, tow line slack

Robert Fulton, more widely acclaimed for his commercial success with the
steamship Clermont, *built the four-man submarine* Nautilus. *Sails provided sur-*
face propulsion and a hand-driven screw propelled the submarine underwater.
(Illustration courtesy of the Submarine Force Library and Museum.)

was taken up and the explosion was triggered by a gunlock. The device was
demonstrated successfully in Brest Harbor, where an old 40-foot sloop was
demolished. Napoleon missed a wonderful opportunity to command the
seas with an exclusive, proven naval advantage when he refused to finance
the construction of larger versions of *Nautilus* to attack British ships. He
may have been influenced by the prevalent attitude of most French naval
officers; they termed underwater warfare unworthy, ungallant, and fit only
for Algerians and pirates.

Fulton protested against the moral objection in a letter to a French
government official: "If at first glance, the means I propose seem revolting,
it is only because they are extraordinary. They are anything but inhuman. . ."

Fulton had gone as far as he could with the French. He then persuaded
England's Prime Minister William Pitt to let him try his torpedoes against
the French. He was not one to play favorites. All he wanted was some
nation to adopt his invention, with only one reservation. His methods of
destruction were never to be used against his own nation, the United States,
unless she used them first.

On the night of October 2, 1805, several of Fulton's 18-foot torpedoes were towed by British ships into Boulogne Harbor. But instead of towing them underwater as designed by Fulton, they were set loose and allowed to drift with the tide to explode on contact. It is a wonder that even one small French vessel with a crew of 21 was destroyed by such primitive mine-laying tactics. The experience did little to prove the worth of Fulton's armament towing concept.

The British lost interest in Fulton's invention when the French fleet was destroyed at Trafalgar on October 21, 1805. First Lord of the Admiralty, Earl St. Vincent, remarked that, "Pitt was the greatest fool that ever existed, to encourage a mode of war which they who commanded the seas did not want, and which, if successful, would deprive them of it." Britain's naval leaders persisted in St. Vincent's attitude for the next hundred years.

War of 1812

Fulton returned to the United States, determined to continue his experiments. During the War of 1812, he built a submarine to be used against the British squadron based at New London, Connecticut. He had claimed that American difficulties were due to European Navies and, "How then is America to prevent this? Certainly not by attempting to build a fleet to cope with the fleets of Europe but if possible by rendering the European fleets

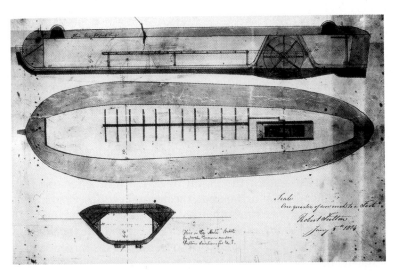

This submarine, Mute, *designed by Fulton in 1814, during the War of 1812, was lost on the north shore of Long Island, New York.* (Illustration courtesy of the Submarine Force Library and Museum.)

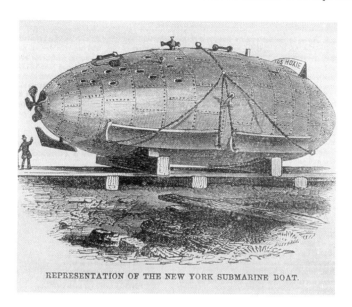

REPRESENTATION OF THE NEW YORK SUBMARINE BOAT.

This submarine, built in New York in 1851, was designed for peaceful purposes such as laying cables and collecting pearls. (Illustration courtesy of the Submarine Force Library and Museum.)

useless." His solution was a new submarine, *Mute*, 80 feet long, with a beam of 21 feet. A steam engine provided surface propulsion so quiet that it led to the vessel's name. Two screw-propellers operated by a winch produced a speed of about four knots submerged. The submarine's hull and top hatch were constructed of eight-inch planking covered with a half-inch of iron armor plating. The hull resembled a conventional boat but the top arched like a turtle shell, leading the British to dub her a "turtle boat."

The submarine was designed to tow five of Fulton's torpedoes. One destroyed a vessel of 200 tons during a test in New York Harbor, assuring Fulton that the boat and armament were ready for a military mission. The submarine left New York on June 19, 1814 and headed down Long Island Sound toward the British ships at New London. Unfortunately, an unpredicted northwest gale blew in the next day. It battered the small vessel, and grounded her at Long Island's Horton Beach, about 12 miles west of Plum Gut. One crew member drowned.

On June 26, H.M.S. *Maidstone* and H.M.S. *Sylph* located the stranded American vessel in the wash of the beach in a small bay, protected by a hastily assembled group of American militiamen. The British raked the beach with cannon fire, dispersing the militia. Then, British Royal Marines commanded by Lieutenant John Bowen of *Maidstone*, stripped the submarine, set charges, and blew her to pieces.

The British newspapers called the American's attempt at underwater warfare "cowardly," "barbarous," and "inhuman." How quickly they had forgotten Fulton's efforts on their behalf. American newspapers, however, quickly reminded the British of their past activities.

Fulton had expected that the submarine would win him fame, but he is still best known for his commercial success with the steamboat, not his contribution to underwater warfare.

Little else of importance to submarine development occurred during the first half of the 19th century. However, a Frenchman named Alexander constructed several submarines in France. In 1851, using Alexander's design, a submarine was built in New York City by the Submarine Exploring Company. The stated purpose of the so-called *New York Submarine Boat,* was to retrieve pearls off Panama. It was reported that the vessel would also be useful for recovering gold from the bottom of rivers and for collecting coral.

The submarine was constructed from strong boiler iron. She was 10 feet in diameter, and 30 feet long. Hinged shelves on the outside held ballast that could be released to allow the submarine to surface. The interior was divided into two compartments; the aft was filled with water for additional ballast, which could be pumped out for buoyancy control. A hand-driven screw propeller was used for propulsion. The boat was reported to be able to remain submerged for seven hours by using a chemical air repurification system. While submerged, telegraphic communication was maintained

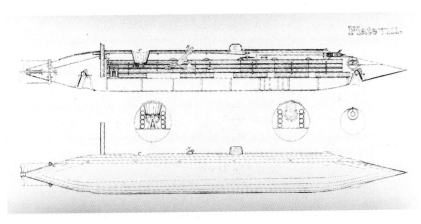

One of Lodner Phillips' submarines, several of which he launched on Lake Michigan. His designs were adapted for use in warfare. (Illustration courtesy of the Naval Historical Center.)

with a support vessel on the surface. Before shipping the submarine to Panama, the builders intended to use it to lay a telegraph line between Brooklyn and Manhattan. The submarine's fate is not known.

Also in 1851, an American shoemaker, Lodner Phillips, launched the first of several submarines on Lake Michigan. He incorporated three important innovations into his design: large volume of compressed air, washing tanks for air purification, and buoyancy control through a pendulum to transfer ballast water fore or aft, as needed.

Civil War

The American Civil War stimulated experimentation on both sides. North and South explored every new concept for waging war more effectively. Explosive bullets, machine guns, breech loading rifles, armored warships, and field telegraph all made their contributions. The Confederates, determined to break the Union Navy's blockade, built several semi-submersible vessels and submarines. The Confederate submarine *H.L. Hunley* was the first underwater vessel to sink an enemy ship in action. However, she herself would sink four times, losing 32 of the 36 men who served on her crews. *Hunley*'s tragic career is covered in Chapter 1.

Some historians have overlooked the federal government's Civil War efforts to develop a submarine. Yet, in the first year of the war, a Frenchman, Brutus de Villeroi designed and built an iron-hulled submarine at Philadelphia. He was well experienced and had constructed a submarine in France 30 years earlier. After emigrating to the United States in 1859, he obtained the backing of a wealthy Philadelphian to build a submarine. The objective was to salvage a British warship, *De Braak,* which had sunk off Lewes, Delaware in 1798, with a cargo of treasure. The submarine was an iron cylinder about 33 feet long and 4 feet at its greatest diameter. Propulsion was by a stern screw. While submerged, the vessel's air could be cleansed by a chemical process.

De Villeroi's submarine attracted the attention of the U.S. Navy. Its feasibility was studied by a board of three naval officers who issued a favorable report on July 7, 1861. The board concluded that the submarine could remain submerged for a considerable time. A chamber in her bow would allow a diver, using tubes attached to the boat, to leave and return while the submarine remained submerged. They speculated that the diver could attach some explosive device to a target ship's hull after leaving the submarine. Even that support failed to influence the Navy to acquire De Villeroi's submarine. After waiting for two months, he wrote to President Lincoln, urging action on the basis that his submarine offered "prompt and decisive results with economy in men and money." On November 1, 1861 a contract for $14,000 authorized him to proceed with production of a larger version of his submarine.

Commodore Joseph Smith, Chief of the Bureau of Yards and Docks, was a strong supporter of the new submarine to counter the Confederate iron-clad, *Merrimac,* then under construction at the Norfolk Navy Yard. His hope was that the Confederate threat might be destroyed before she was completed. However, construction problems delayed launching De Villeroi's submarine *Alligator* (also known as *Submarine Propeller*) until April 30, 1862. By that time, *Merrimac* had wreaked havoc on the Union fleet.

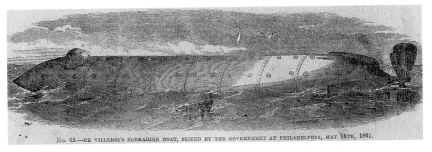

NO. 62.—DE VILLEROI'S SUBMARINE BOAT, SEIZED BY THE GOVERNMENT AT PHILADELPHIA, MAY 16TH, 1861.

De Villeroi's submarine Submarine Propeller (Alligator) *was built during the Civil War for the Union Navy.* (Illustration courtesy of the Naval Historical Center.)

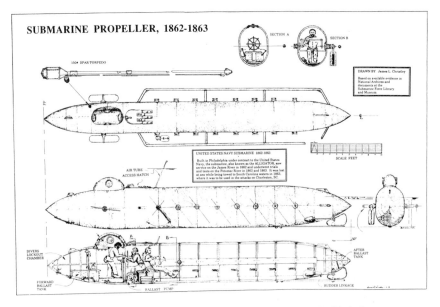

Illustration of Submarine Propeller (Alligator) *by James J. Christley.*

The new submarine measured 47 feet in length, with a 4-foot 6-inch beam, displaced 275 tons on the surface and 350 tons submerged, and carried a crew of 20. Near the bow was a round dome with four ports for underwater vision. Just aft of the dome was the access hatch. Propulsion, on the surface or submerged, was by 16 oars. They were replaced within several months by a hand-turned screw propeller. Then the submarine was towed to Hampton Roads, with orders to demolish the Petersburg Bridge across the Appomattox River. However, Commodore Goldsborough, commanding officer at Hampton Roads, canceled the project. He informed Gideon Welles, secretary of the navy, that *Alligator* was unsuited to the task. When awash, the submarine drew six feet of water. To disgorge men through the bottom of her hull for the demolition task would require at least two feet of water under the hull. Even in eight feet of water, the upper part of the submarine would be exposed to the enemy. The shallow Appomattox, with its narrows and strong current, was no place for *Alligator*. After a brief stay at Hampton Roads, the submarine returned to the Washington Navy Yard.

Alligator was the only Union submarine launched during the Civil War, but was not commissioned into the navy. She was commanded by a civilian, S. Eakin, during her early career. With a U.S. Navy officer and crew assigned to the submarine, she was taken in tow by U.S.S. *Sumpter,* and departed for Charleston, South Carolina. On April 2, 1863, the vessels ran into a storm and *Alligator* had to be cut adrift. She was never seen again, and was presumed lost off Cape Hatteras.

Pascal Plant of Washington, D.C., produced a rocket-driven torpedo, the first recorded self-propelled torpedo. Secretary of the Navy Gideon Welles witnessed a test at the Washington Navy Yard in 1862. Two torpedoes were fired from a test platform at a stationary target. One struck a mudbank and the other veered off course and sank a small schooner, *Diana,* anchored nearby. The test resulted in the first sinking of a vessel— unfortunately the wrong vessel—by a self-propelled torpedo.

The following month another test resulted in a torpedo soaring into the air about 20 feet from its launching site, and being airborne for 100 yards before splashing down. The naval observers, not realizing the significance of the potential weapon, left in disgust.

Six years later, a British engineer, Robert Whitehead, and an Austrian naval officer, Captain Luppis, developed a torpedo propelled by compressed air. Later, two counter rotating screw-propellers were added to hold the torpedo on course. Those torpedoes were eventually adopted by all navies.

The war ended, but submarine development had gained momentum from the interest of both North and South in the potential strength of a Navy supported by effective underwater vessels.

Halstead's Intelligent Whale *at the New York (Brooklyn) Navy Yard in 1915. Thirty-nine men lost their lives in this submarine. Today the vessel is at the Naval Museum at the Washington Navy Yard.* (Photo courtesy of the Submarine Force Library and Museum.)

O.S. Halstead's submarine, *Intelligent Whale,* was sponsored by the U.S. Navy. She proved to be a success on her first trial in 1872. In subsequent dives however, three crews, a total of 39 men, were lost, and the submarine was abandoned. For many years, *Intelligent Whale* was displayed in front of the Brooklyn Navy Yard. She can be seen today at the naval museum at the Washington Navy Yard.

John Holland

In 1875, an Irish immigrant, John P. Holland, submitted plans for his submarine to the U.S. Navy. But too little time had elapsed since the tragic experiences of the Confederate submarine *Hunley* and the U.S. Navy's own *Intelligent Whale.* Holland's plans were rejected on the basis that no intelligent man could be persuaded to serve in such a craft.

Holland was not dissuaded. He struck off on his own and built his first submarine in 1878, financed by the Fenian Brotherhood, a group working for the independence of Ireland. The boat was designed for operation by one man wearing a self-contained diving suit. Submergence was controlled by mid-ship hydroplanes, and the vessel was powered by a four-horsepower gasoline engine. Holland could not get the submerged control to work satisfactorily, and abandoned the $4,000 project.

Three years later, Holland launched his second boat, again financed by his Irish associates. The cost was $18,000 exclusive of an engine or other operating machinery. The *New York Sun* referred to the new submarine as *Fenian Ram* and the name stuck with the 31-foot, 17-1/2 ton vessel. The boat operated with stern instead of mid-ship hydroplanes, for improved control underwater. The single screw was operated by a 16-horsepower gasoline engine. While underwater, the engine received air from the boat's interior and exhausted the fumes through a valve in the hull. An 11-foot pneumatic bow tube to fire a six-foot projectile while submerged provided armament.

Dissention in the Fenian Brotherhood led to confiscation of *Fenian Ram* by members, ending Holland's association with the vessel. Holland then turned to a company promoted by Lieutenant Edward Zalinsky of the Fifth U.S. Artillery. Zalinsky had been experimenting with dynamite guns for years. The concept of fitting an underwater vessel with a pneumatic gun for firing large dynamite charges intrigued him, and he backed Holland in

Inside Holland's Fenian Ram. (Photo courtesy of the Submarine Force Library and Museum.)

building a 50-foot submarine. The new boat included an innovative camera tube periscope and the pneumatic gun the artillery lieutenant wanted. But as the new submarine was launched, her iron hull plates separated; she sank to the bottom and was never raised.

Holland was disappointed, but not defeated. He and another American, Simon Lake, with a strikingly different background, were together responsible for the development and perfection of the early submarine. Lake was moved by visions of adventure and exploration beneath the sea; Holland saw the submarine as an instrument of war in an increasingly tense world. Though the competition between the two was often heated, they inevitably influenced each other—and the entire course of submarine history.

Simon Lake

Lake, born in 1866, spent his boyhood in the bucolic surroundings of Pleasantville, New Jersey. Around 1880, the schoolboy read Jules Verne's sensational new book *20,000 Leagues Under the Sea.* The teenager's imagination was so fired by this experience that he immediately experimented with his own "submarine," turning a canvas canoe upside down for submerged floating in a nearby river.

Submarine inventor Simon Lake was moved by visions of adventure and exploration beneath the sea, not warfare. (Photo courtesy of the Naval Historical Center.)

Simon Lake envisioned his submarines being used for peaceful endeavors, such as salvaging sunken ships. (Illustration courtesy of the Submarine Force Library and Museum.)

Argonaut, *Lake's first major submarine, was 36 feet long, with a 9-foot beam, and a 30 horsepower gasoline engine. The large toothed wheels were for moving along the bottom. The open door under the bow would allow a diver to leave the submarine, with a long air hose, and search the surrounding sea floor.* (Photo courtesy of the Submarine Force Library and Museum.)

Lake retained a boyish sense of curiosity and adventure throughout his career. His company built submarines for the world's navies, but Lake believed that the submarine's greatest potential lay in the area of underwater exploration, salvage, construction, and mining.

In 1897, Lake built *Argonaut*—his first major submarine. The boat was the first to have a double hull, with the space between the two hulls used for buoyancy tanks. Two 10-foot-high, solid cast-iron wheels were mounted under the hull. A smaller, pivotable wheel was attached to the stern. *Argonaut* sailed from Norfolk to New York in 1898, the first submarine to navigate extensively in open waters. That major step in submarine development made headlines worldwide and prompted congratulations from the aging Jules Verne. Lake considered this accolade one of the high points of his life.

Professor Josiah H.L. Tuck launched his first submarine, *Tuck I,* in 1884. The electrically powered craft required a diver in a pressure suit to guide it. Tuck's second design, *Peacemaker,* was launched the following year. It produced steam for propulsion from a solution of caustic soda, and survived several short trips up the Hudson River before it was abandoned.

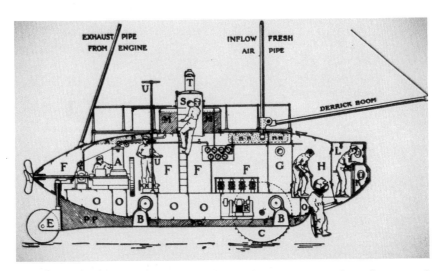

Five men, including Lake, made a cruise of more than 2,000 miles in Argonaut, *in 1898. A diver can be seen leaving through the open hatch in the submarine's bow.* (Illustration courtesy of the Submarine Force Library and Museum.)

William C. Whitney, secretary of the U.S. Navy, obtained an appropriation of $150,000 in 1888 to finance submarine construction. Several submarine inventors, including John Holland responded to the request for bids. Holland's was accepted in 1889, but a change in administration and a new secretary of the navy cancelled the contract.

Simon Lake, then of Atlantic Highlands, New Jersey, introduced a tiny one-man submarine *Argonaut Jr.,* in 1895. Unable to acquire funding,

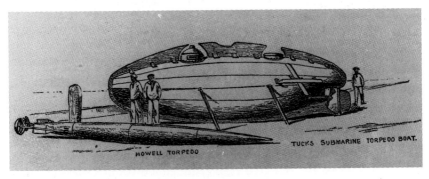

Tuck's electrically powered submarine, launched in 1884, required a diver in a pressure suit to operate the vessel. (Illustration courtesy of the Naval Historical Center.)

Lake designed the vessel so that he could build it himself inexpensively. Lake's aunt advanced him the money for materials, and his cousin helped him build the submarine. Hand-cranked wheels provided propulsion along the bottom. A soda fountain tank was used for compressed air, and a plumber's hand pump emptied the water ballast tanks. The submarine was designed to dive to a depth of only 20 feet.

Lake continued to be influenced by Verne's *20,000 Leagues Under the Sea*. His first submarine design was a distant cry from Captain Nemo's fictitious *Nautilus*. But, like *Nautilus* and De Villeroi's *Alligator* of the Civil War, the submarine did include an air lock for a diver to leave the boat to explore the surrounding bottom.

During President Cleveland's second administration (1893-97), a study of submarine development led to the appropriation of $200,000 for submarine construction. A request for bids in 1895 drew new designs from eight bidders, including Holland, Lake, and Tuck.

Holland again won the bid, and received a $150,000 contract to build a submarine for the U.S. Navy. It was to be Holland's eighth submarine,

Lake's Argonaut Jr. *was only 14 feet long and about 5 feet high, with a beam of 4½ feet. She was constructed of yellow pine timber, and could be propelled along the bottom by hand-cranked wheels.* (Photo courtesy of the Submarine Force Library and Museum.)

Plunger, 85 feet long, 11 feet 6 inches in diameter and 165 tons displacement while submerged. A gasoline-fired boiler of 1,500-horsepower driving two screws provided surface transportation. Electric motors and storage batteries were used for submerged propulsion. The design called for a speed of 15 knots surfaced and 8 knots submerged. Downhaul screws and diving hydroplanes were to be installed for vertical control while submerged.

The vessel was completed in 1897, but government specifications, including steam propulsion for surface running, were so rigid and unrealistic that Holland knew *Plunger* would probably fail her tests. He realized that such a failure would exclude the Holland Torpedo Boat Company from further government contract consideration unless an immediate successor could interest the Navy. He persuaded his business associates to let him design and build a follow-on submarine strictly in accordance with his own ideas. As Holland expected, *Plunger* did fail her acceptance tests. Excessive heat developed by the boiler was a major factor.

Holland was convinced that *Plunger* was too long. He reduced the dimensions of his new submarine, *Holland,* to 53 feet 10 inches long, 10 feet 3 inches diameter, and 74 tons submerged displacement. A single, 50-horsepower Otto gasoline engine provided propulsion while surfaced, and a 50-horsepower electric motor drove the submarine while submerged. Storage batteries operated the electric motor. They were rechargeable, but their 60 cells provided only a 50-mile submerged range before recharging was required.

Holland ran at eight knots on the surface and five knots submerged. Her radius was 1,500 miles surfaced. Diving control was accomplished with stern hydroplanes that could be manually operated or coupled with air compressors for automatic control. The compressors also operated the vertical rudders. Tanks were installed for fresh air storage.

The conning tower was originally planned to be telescopic, but the plans were changed and a fixed conning tower was fitted. Armament consisted of a bow tube, for three short Whitehead torpedoes (Whitehead had developed his self-propelled torpedoes in England) and a pneumatic dynamite gun, also in the bow.

Holland's career started ignominiously; she flooded and sank while still at dockside at Crescent Shipyard, Elizabethport, New Jersey. She was raised and made her first successful run on March 17, 1898. The Navy Department inspected the submarine and, though the report was encouraging, it concluded that *Holland* was not yet satisfactory. After alterations were made, the boat was again tested in April.

On one trial run, the crew was overcome by gasoline engine exhaust fumes, an occasional submarine problem until the diesel engine was introduced.

Holland was resubmitted for Navy tests on November 6, 1898; then, she was transferred to Washington for inspection and further tests. Assistant

John P. Holland prepares to climb out of U.S.S. Holland's *(SS-1) conning tower. He saw the submarine as an instrument of war.* (Photo courtesy of the Submarine Force Library and Museum.)

This 54-foot, 64-ton submarine, designed by John Holland, is being placed in the water at Greenport, Long Island, in 1899. The following year she was commissioned into the U.S. Navy as U.S.S. Holland *(SS-1).* (Photo courtesy of the Naval Historical Center.)

Secretary of the Navy Theodore Roosevelt stated, "Sometimes the *Holland* doesn't work perfectly but when she does, and I don't think that . . . we can afford to let her slip."

Additional successful Navy trials took place on March 14, 1900 before Admiral George Dewey. Based on that performance, the submarine was accepted on April 11, 1900 at a cost of $150,000. The Navy's next seven submarines, the A boats, became an international standard. Holland's company sold patents to several countries including Japan and Great Britain. At the height of Holland's success, his company was absorbed by the Electric Boat Company of New Suffolk, New York. Holland's power in the company slowly eroded. The methods of 20th-century business were of little interest to the 19th-century inventor. He died in 1914.

U.S.S. *Holland* received designation as hull number 1, first of a list that would approach 300 before World War II. Her crew of five enlisted men was under command of Lieutenant Harry H. Caldwell. The submarine never saw action. She was used primarily as a training boat at Annapolis for 17 years of service.

Holland could stay submerged for only relatively short periods. Aside from that limitation, she incorporated six basic concepts that were vital for further submarine development:

1. Internal combustion engine for surface propulsion.
2. Electric motors for submerged power.

Holland's *first crew*. (Photo courtesy of the Submarine Force Library and Museum.)

General plans of inboard profile and decks of Holland. (Illustration courtesy of the Naval Historical Center.)

3. Storage batteries.
4. Normal buoyancy.
5. Immovable center of gravity.
6. Control in vertical plane.

Until Holland entered the field, submarine emphasis was focused on the principle of altering buoyancy to regulate position beneath the surface. It was known that a vessel displaced its weight in water and it would sink if ballast increased its weight to more than the weight of water displaced. Hence, many earlier submarines were designed to float as surface vessels, and were made to descend by flooding the ballast tanks. The capacity of the ballast reservoir was carefully calculated to provide the boat with little positive buoyancy when it was filled. A screw propeller on a vertical shaft

Holland *underway in Long Island Sound.* (Photo courtesy of the Submarine Force Library and Museum.)

The tiny Holland *is dwarfed by the Russian battleship* Retvizan *as both enter the dry dock at the New York Navy Yard. The battleship was later sunk in the Russo-Japanese War.* (Photo courtesy of the Submarine Force Library and Museum.)

controlled the submarine from sinking further than intended, or buoyancy was changed by pumping water in or out of the ballast reservoir.

Holland's new design provided assurance that when the ballast tanks were filled, the submarine would retain a small amount of positive buoyancy; there could be no further changes in water ballast, thus fixing an immovable center of gravity. Control in the vertical plane (depth) was by horizontal rudders (hydroplanes) and the power plant; control in the horizontal plane was by means of a vertical rudder and the power plant.

Success of the *Holland* led to a Navy appropriation for six additional submarines at a cost of $170,000 each. *Plunger* was redesigned and was accepted into the Navy.

In 1901, Holland launched a larger submarine, *Fulton,* which was eventually sold to Russia. The Japanese purchased five boats of the same design. The British also ordered plans, so they could build five submarines on their own.

Holland launched his last submarine in 1906, before he was maneuvered out of what had become the Electric Boat Company. *Octopus* was 105 feet long, with a diameter of 14 feet, and a submerged displacement of 275 tons. Surface speed reached 11 knots, and when submerged, the boat could cruise at almost 10 knots. Armament was two torpedo tubes and five torpedoes. She was designed to carry her 15-man crew to a depth of 200 feet.

Simon Lake's first submarine for the U.S. Navy was *G-1* (SS-*19 1/2*, see Chapter 2). The 161-foot long, 516-ton boat was launched in 1911. Gasoline engines produced a speed of 14 knots for surface propulsion and electric motors produced 10 knots submerged.

John Holland's designs and those of Simon Lake developed into conflicting submarine prototypes in the United States that lasted for decades. Two fundamental design differences distinguished Holland and Lake boats. Holland used ballast tanks inside a single pressure hull while Lake ballast tanks were sandwiched between an inner pressure hull and an outer hull. Secondly, Holland submarines dove at an angle while Lake's submerged with little or no angle. Each had its share of supporters within the Navy. Eventually, Lake's design was adopted, but the dichotomy hindered U.S. submarine design for years.

American submarine progress was steady from 1900 to 1914 despite the design conflicts. Diesel propulsion was adopted in 1905. Twenty submarines were completed for the Navy by 1911, the largest 516 tons. By 1914, 25 submarines had been accepted. Those early submarines were not intended for extended cruises, perhaps a reflection of early assessment of the submarine as a weapon of defense. However, U.S.S. *Skipjack* (SS-*24*), an E-class, was the first U.S. Navy submarine to make an Atlantic crossing. It was in 1917.

World War I

When the country entered World War I, the latest submarine in the U.S. fleet of 30 was the L-class. It was about 167 feet long, had a submerged displacement of 548 tons, a crew of two officers and 26 enlisted men, and a submerged speed of 10 1/2 knots. Although 20 submarines reached the war zone, none played a major role in combat.

After World War I, coastal defense O- and R-class boats were produced. The O-class was about 630 tons submerged, 172 feet long, with an 18-foot beam. R boats were 50 tons larger, 14 feet longer, and had the same 18-foot beam. Their maximum cruising range was 3,500 miles with a surfaced speed of 14 knots and 10 knots submerged. They were driven by twin diesel engines.

S-class boats followed during the early 1920s. They ranged from 207 to 240 feet long, with a beam of about 20 feet, and submerged displacement of 977-1,230 tons. The development of increasingly powerful depth charges after World War I made it essential to provide stronger hulls. The S boats were refitted and newer type submarines were built for greater depth, with engines to produce faster speeds, and improved escape mechanisms.

Additional types varying from 1,000 to 2,424 tons submerged displacement were constructed from the late 1920s to 1939, including the 1938 fleet type Gato-class with an all-welded hull. The fleet type submarine had a cruising range of 12,000 miles and 20 knots surface speed. It was larger than earlier classes, with a crew of 6 officers and 54 enlisted men. Armament consisted of 10 torpedo tubes, 24 torpedoes, one 3-inch deck gun, two .50 caliber and two .30 caliber machine guns. The U.S. Navy had transformed the submarine service from coastal defense to an oceanic attack force.

World War II

When the Japanese struck Pearl Harbor, 111 U.S. Navy submarines were in service—mainly O-, R- and S-class. During the war, their total was as high as 247. U.S. submarines conducted 1,682 patrols during World War II, of which all but 112 were in the Pacific. At the end of the war there were 200 fleet boats in commission, compared to 46 at the beginning. American submarines sank 1,750 Japanese merchant ships and more than 200 major warships. The toll accounted for 56% of all Japanese naval and merchant shipping. The submarine force was one of the major instruments of victory. World War II losses were 52 U.S. submarines and 3,505 men, 16% of all officers and 13% of all enlisted Submarine Service personnel.

Although proportionately greater than other branches of the U.S. armed forces, those losses were markedly lower than the 85 Italian, 130 Japanese, and 781 German U-boats sunk.

Development of the American submarine was slow and frequently disastrous. Progress was hindered by competing design theory and the absence of a central, driving force such as Germany's wartime naval isolation and the urgency of disrupting Allied shipping. The superiority of U.S. submarine performance evidenced by their achievements and lower loss ratios than the enemy during World War II did not stem from basic submarine design, so much as two other factors—American submarines were fitted with radar for offense and defense and Axis submarines were constantly harassed by Allied aircraft.

After World War II, fleet submarines were upgraded with high-capacity storage batteries, streamlined hulls, and the German U-boat snorkel breather for prolonged underwater cruises while using diesel engines. However, the famous fleet boats of World War II became obsolete with the introduction of missile-firing nuclear-powered submarines. John Holland's Electric Boat Company built the first nuclear submarine *Nautilus,* which was launched in 1955. Faster attack submarines, cargo carriers, troop transports and guided missile launchers have enhanced the image of the submarine as a formidable warship.

The Future

Nuclear power has expanded the role of large submarines in the navies of the world. Great powers may never again confront one another in naval combat, a welcome prospect. But if naval conflict occurs, the submarine will play a more decisive role than ever before. In both World Wars I and II, the outcome was in precarious balance while Germany controlled the Atlantic sea lanes with her U-boats. Learned observers have speculated that with more U-boats Germany could have starved Britain into submission. Winston Churchill termed the "Battle of the Atlantic" one of the most decisive conflicts in the history of warfare. He wrote in *The Second World War,* "The only thing that ever really frightened me during the war was the U-boat peril . . . I was even more anxious about this battle than I had been about the glorious air fight called the "Battle of Britain."

After 2,500 years of wooden warships, an era that ended abruptly in the 19th century, the mighty battleship that dominated the naval scene for 50 years has been succeeded by the aircraft carrier. Those lofty floating superstructures in turn may be displaced by long-range underwater warships in deciding the balance of power in the navies of tomorrow.

Left to right, Miss Marguerite Holland, daughter of John Holland; Mrs. Frederick Hirons, great-great-great-grandniece of David Bushnell; John Hopkins, president of General Dynamics Corp.; Thomas Lake, son of Simon Lake; and Mrs. David Selden, great-great-grandniece of Robert Fulton. The occasion for the gathering was the dedication of the Submarine Library at the Electric Boat Division of General Dynamics Corp. in Groton, Connecticut on April 11, 1955. (Photo courtesy of the Submarine Force Library and Museum.)

CHAPTER 1

H.L. Hunley—
First Sub to Sink an Enemy Ship

Location: Charleston, South Carolina, exact location unknown
Approximate depth of water: probably shallow
Visibility: probably bad
Current: moderate to strong
Access: unknown, probably boat

The American Civil War stimulated experimentation by North and South, exploring every new concept for waging war more effectively. Explosive bullets, machine guns, breech loading rifles, armored ships and field telegraph were in the forefront. The Confederates, determined to break the Union Navy's blockade, built several semi-submersible warships. They operated partially submerged, but always with part of the upper structure above water. Their low silhouettes and the small targets they presented to Union gunners provided an effective defense. The vessels, usually cylindrical, were either hand cranked or steam propeller driven. Because they were so much smaller than the Union vessels they confronted, they were called "Davids," against the enemy Goliath. Armament consisted of spar-torpedoes, explosive charges fixed to the end of an 18-foot pole projecting from the bow. One of the "Davids," armed with such a spar-

A Confederate "David" torpedo-boat aground at low tide at Charleston Harbor about 1865. Steam-powered semi-submersibles like this one were intended to break the Union blockade. (Photo courtesy of the Naval Historical Center.)

torpedo, attacked the Union ironclad *New Ironsides* in Charleston Harbor, damaging but not sinking her. The formidable Union warship was put out of action for a year. Rear Admiral John A. Dahlgren, U.S.N., commander of the blockading squadron on the south Atlantic coast, threatened to hang the crew of the "David," "for using an engine of war not recognized by civilized nations." Dahlgren, however, urged Secretary of War Gideon Welles to launch "reprisals in kind." Welles replied, "The Department concurs." Later in the war C.S.S. *Albermarle* was sunk by a Union torpedo ram.

Early in 1862, *Pioneer,* a Confederate privateer submarine, was built in New Orleans by James K. Scott, Robert H. Barrow, Baxter Watson, and James R. McClintock. The submarine was 34 feet long with a beam of 4 feet and a displacement of 4 tons. She was manned by a crew of two or more and propelled by a hand-driven screw. Her only armament was a mine-like cannister loaded with explosives. Before *Pioneer* could go into action, a Union fleet advanced on New Orleans, and the submarine was scuttled in Lake Ponchartrain to prevent her capture. In 1878, a young boy swimming in the lake discovered the submarine. *Pioneer* was raised to lie rusting as a lakeside exhibit for a generation. She was then moved to the state home for Confederate soldiers. When that facility closed, the submarine was given to the Louisiana State Museum, and is now on display in the arcade of the *Presbytère,* in New Orleans.

Undeterred by the loss of *Pioneer,* two of her inventors, McClintock and Watson, built a second submarine with assistance from Horace L. Hunley, a Louisiana lawyer and plantation owner. The effort was funded by the Confederate Army; construction was by Park and Lyons, a machine shop in Mobile, Alabama. The boat was about 25 feet long with a beam of 5 feet. Like her predecessor, propulsion was manually accomplished by hand-turned screw. And like her predecessor, she was never to see action. The

The Confederate privateer submarine Pioneer *on exhibit in 1926 at the state home for Confederate soldiers in New Orleans. Now the property of the Louisiana State Museum, she is on display in the arcade of the* Presbytère *in New Orleans.* (Photo courtesy of the Naval Historical Center.)

vessel was lost to the Confederate cause when she foundered in Mobile Bay, this time without loss of life. After that failure, the Confederate Army withdrew financial support. Not deterred, Hunley used his personal funds to construct another submarine, *American Diver.*

The new submarine was also constructed at Park and Lyons. *American Diver* was actually a modified 25-foot long steam boiler, cut lengthwise into two pieces, with a 9-foot iron section riveted between the two halves. Depth was 5 feet, and with ballast tanks, bow, and stern added, the length was about 35 feet and the beam was 4 feet. Propulsion was by a hand-driven screw-propeller that provided a maximum speed of four knots under ideal conditions. The submarine carried a complement of nine men. A steel crankshaft running the length of the boat was manually turned by eight men. The captain sat in the bow to control the steering and diving hydroplanes. Ballast tanks in the bow and stern were flooded by sea cocks and drained with pumps. The iron keel was mounted to permit quick release for rapid ascent.

The submarine's tragic career included sinking four times, losing 32 of the 36 men who served on her crews and the death of Hunley. She was distinguished as the first submarine to sink an enemy ship, although she was only partially submerged during the attack.

General P.T. Beauregard believed that the "Davids" and the new submarine could neutralize the Union blockade. He predicted, "they are destined ere long to change the system of naval warfare." Beauregard ordered *American Diver* to be shipped by rail to Charleston, South Carolina, for trials in Charleston Harbor. They convinced him that the civilian crew was

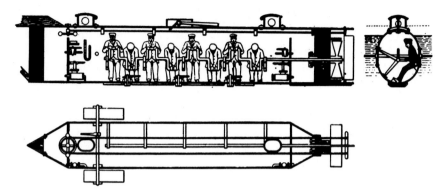

Cutaway plans of H.L. Hunley, *showing her 8-man manual propulsion system.* (Illustration courtesy of the Naval Historical Center.)

too timid for war action. He installed an all-volunteer Navy crew commanded by Lieutenant John Payne, from Alabama.

Disaster

American Diver was ordered out on a trial run shortly after the new crew took over. She was moored behind the steamer *Etiwan* with Lieutenant Payne standing in the forward hatch. As the submarine left her mooring and moved past *Etiwan,* Payne became entangled in a cable hanging from the steamer's stern. Struggling to free himself, he stepped on the hydroplane controls, and sent the submarine into an immediate dive. Water poured down the open hatch, rushing past Payne and his second in command, Lieutenant Charles Hasker, who was positioned on the crank shaft directly behind Payne.

As the submarine started under, Hasker forced his way up through the hatch against the pressure of the inrushing water. Just before he was clear of the hatch the cover closed on his leg, trapping him, while the submarine settled to the bottom. Fortunately, the water was shallow, and Hasker managed to free his almost severed leg and swim to the surface. Only he and Payne survived. The rest of the crew were trapped inside, and drowned.

After the submarine was raised by divers, a second volunteer crew was mustered. Lieutenant Payne retained command, but Hasker remained hospitalized, a misfortune that saved his life.

The submarine was readied for another trial run to prove her worth to the South's war effort. The test run began with the submarine underway on the surface and both forward and aft hatches open. Again, Payne stood forward; his second officer stood in the aft hatch. With very little freeboard, both hatches were exposed to the risk of swamping in heavy seas; they projected only eight inches above the deck. The prevailing calm seas presented no problem as the trial progressed. Then, the submarine's tragic history was repeated as the bow wave of a passing ship washed over her low hatches. Water rushed in, and she quickly sank. Only Payne and his second officer escaped death.

With two tragedies under military crews, Horace Hunley was granted approval to operate his submarine with a civilian crew after divers raised the submarine—for the second time. Several trials followed without incident. Emphasis was placed on diving under a target ship, then surfacing to drag a torpedo against the target's hull. On one such trial, Hunley was at the controls in a dive under the Confederate warship *Indian Chief,* which was moored in the Cooper River. It was the morning of October 10, 1863; sailors aboard *Indian Chief* followed the line of bubbles that streamed to the surface as Hunley approached from the port side. After the bubbles disappeared under their ship, they rushed to the starboard rail, but the submarine failed to surface. She had sunk for the third time.

A week later, the submarine was raised and examined to determine why she sank. Investigation found Horace Hunley's body at the forward hatch with the broken handle for the bow ballast tank sea cock at his feet. When his efforts to close the sea cock failed, he had tried to escape through the hatch, but water pressure prevented him from opening it. He died when air ran out. The recovered submarine was renamed *H.L. Hunley.*

In its toll of lives, *Hunley* was providing better service to the Union than the Confederacy. General Beauregard, who had already acknowledged that the submarine effort would have to be abandoned, was approached by two

Horace L. Hunley, who was lost on October 15, 1863 when the manually powered Confederate submarine Am-erican Diver did not surface after a dive in Charleston Harbor. After the sub-marine was raised and refitted she was named H.L. Hunley *in his honor.* (Photo courtesy of the Naval Historical Center.)

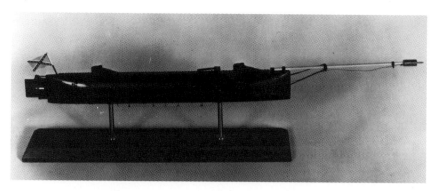

A ship model of Hunley *carrying a version of the Confederate flag. Note the spar, with an explosive charge attached to its tip, protruding from her bow.* (Photo courtesy of the Naval Historical Center.)

artillery engineers, Lieutenants George E. Dixon and W.A. Alexander, from the 21st Alabama Volunteers. Both had been assigned to the Mobile machine shop where *Hunley* was built. Beauregard granted them approval for another attempt, stipulating that the boat only be operated awash like the Davids, never totally submerged. This precluded diving under a victim. A spar-torpedo explosive charge, like those used on the Davids, was fixed to the end of a 10-foot pole and attached to the bow. It was agreed that *Hunley* would ram her opponent, exploding the torpedo by impact.

Several of the new volunteer crew had witnessed *Hunley's* disaster from the deck of *Indian Chief*. Still, they were willing to serve aboard her. Their faith seemed well founded when, at about 9 p.m. on February 17, 1864, *Hunley* sortied from Breach Inlet to a point two and a half miles off Charleston and sank the 13-gun, 1,240-ton Union blockader U.S.S. *Housatonic*. It was the first sinking of a vessel by a submarine in action.

Like the earlier David's damage to U.S.S. *New Ironsides, Hunley* had accomplished her feat as a semi-submersible, using a ram type spar-torpedo. The lookout on *Housatonic* spotted a log-like object moving through the water and reported it to the bridge. The crew was called to quarters, the anchor cable slipped, and the ship's engine reversed. The Confederate submarine's spar-torpedo struck the Union warship on the starboard side. The explosion blew the stern off the steamer. Had the steam-sloop *Housatonic* moved ahead instead of back when she slipped her cable, she might have escaped destruction.

Housatonic sank rapidly after she was hit. *Hunley's* fate is not on record. It is only known that she failed to return from her historic mission. The Confederate submarine may have gone to the bottom with her target, carried into the wreckage by the suction of inrushing water or her own

Above: A Civil War artist's rendering of the Confederate Navy's H.L. Hunley, *the first submarine to sink a ship in action. Below: In 1864, she sank the Union warship* Housatonic. (Illustration and photo courtesy of the Naval Historical Center.)

momentum. Did the explosion destroy *Hunley?* Lieutenant Colonel O.M. Dantzler, commanding an artillery battery at Sullivan's Island, claimed to have exchanged prearranged signals with the Confederate submarine after the attack. If Lieutenant Dixon had opened *Hunley*'s hatch to send that signal, the submarine might have flooded as she had on a previous trial run.

Dixon and his entire Confederate crew were lost with the submarine, while only five Union crewmen were lost on the warship. *Hunley*'s death toll during her disastrous career was more than six times greater than the five lives she exacted from the Union Navy. However, the Confederate projects to develop semi-submersible vessels and submarines kept the Union Navy in a constant state of unrest. By the war's end Confederate underwater warfare, mines, torpedoes, Davids, and *Hunley,* accounted for 29 vessels sunk and 14 damaged. That was more than the rest of the Confederate Navy could claim.

Search for *Hunley*

In 1864, the U.S. Navy examined the wreck of *Housatonic* and dragged an area 500 yards around the wreck site, but did not find *Hunley*. After the war Navy divers moved *Housatonic* to clear the North Channel. However, the warship was still deemed to be a navigational hazard, and was destroyed with dynamite to a level of 20 feet below low water. The divers reported seeing *Hunley* lying nearby and one diver said he touched the submarine's propeller. In 1909, William H. Virden was awarded a contract to remove the wreck. His attempt failed, but he did manage to reduce it to the required depth of 27 feet below mean low water. Years later, when the Army Corps of Engineers dredged a ship channel, *Housatonic* was again blasted with dynamite and dragged away from the proposed channel. Her remains now lie between 6 and 12 feet below the surface in about 26 feet of water.

In July 1980, the National Underwater and Marine Agency, Inc. (NUMA) initiated a search for *Hunley*. The private organization's aim is the preservation of America's maritime heritage by locating and identifying historically significant wrecks. The search for the Confederate submarine was based on the assumption that she sank returning to Breach Inlet. The search area that was selected extended from the point of *Hunley's* departure to the original *Housatonic* wreck site and the submarine's intended return. A 38-foot vessel with a sub-bottom profiler and a small rubber boat equipped with a proton magnetometer were used in the search. The remains of *Housatonic* and four *Hunley*-sized objects were located in the offshore search area and one small one showed up in the inshore area.

In June 1981, NUMA, collaborated with the Institute of Archaeology and Anthropology of the University of South Carolina, in an extended search of the same area. Seventeen consecutive days of running 30-meter wide search lanes parallel to the South Carolina shore produced 19 possible *Hunley* wreck sites. Four were promising enough to warrant investigation, three by probing the bottom, one by airlifting. A total of 59 dives, with 39 hours and 25 minutes underwater, produced nothing. Diving conditions were generally poor and visibility averaged only one to two feet. Strong bottom currents made the survey and airlifting difficult.

A map of the approaches to Charleston, South Carolina, showing positions of wrecks of U.S. ships including Housatonic. *The map was redrawn from "Official Records of the Union and Confederate Navies..."* (Illustration courtesy of the Naval Historical Center.)

Hunley was not found, but somewhere off the South Carolina coast the historic Confederate submarine came to rest after her moment of glory. She was counter-productive in the cause she served for most of her career, but she emerged from those failures like a phoenix from the flames. Her final act was a naval success from which she has not yet returned. Perhaps one day she will, as an historic artifact that future generations may refer to as, "A preserved part of the first submarine to sink an enemy ship in action," and until World War II the only American submarine to sink an enemy vessel.

CHAPTER 2

G Boats—
Lake's First U.S. Navy Subs

G-1
Location: Newport, Rhode Island
Approximate depth of water: 105 feet
Visibility: bad, better at the end of a flood tide
Current: moderate to strong
Access: boat

G-2
Location: Niantic Bay, Connecticut
Approximate depth of water: 75 feet
Visibility: poor, better at the end of a flood tide
Current: moderate to strong, dive at slack tide

Holland (SS-*1*), commissioned in 1900, was the first submarine to be commissioned into the U.S. Navy. De Villeroi's *Alligator* was completed in 1862 and served in the Civil War, but she was never commissioned. *Holland* was 53 feet 10 inches long and displaced 64 tons on the surface, 74 tons submerged. She was powered by a gasoline engine that produced eight knots on the surface and five knots while submerged. Her armament included one torpedo tube and an eight-inch "dynamite" gun.

The next seven U.S. Navy submarines, A-class boats, were also designed and built by John Holland. They, like *Holland,* were shaped like fat teardrops, and were ten feet longer and double the tonnage displacement. They were armed with one torpedo tube, but the "dynamite" gun was abandoned.

Three B-class boats were built by Holland. They were 145 tons surface displacement and 173 tons submerged, 82 feet 5 inches long and armed with two torpedo tubes.

Another Holland design was adopted for five C-class submarines that were nearly three times as large as the A boats and could make 10 1/2 knots on the surface.

Holland continued his monopoly of submarine construction for the U.S. Navy with three D-class boats. They were 134 feet 10 inches long, displaced

Simon Lake, unable to sell Protector *to the U.S. Navy, sold the 65-foot, 130-ton submarine to Russia. Above: A diagram of the submarine's interior. Below:* Protector *running at full speed.* (Illustration and photo courtesy of the Submarine Force Library and Museum.)

288 tons on the surface and 337 tons submerged. Their gasoline engines could produce 13 knots on the surface and 9 1/2 knots submerged. Armament was increased to four torpedo tubes.

Simon Lake arrived on the scene with the G-class submarines. He was one of the most distinguished American pioneers of underwater naval architecture, the inventor of even-keel type submarines. Lake's and Holland's submarine designs differed in many respects. One difference was that Holland boats dove by angling downward, then being pushed under by the force of her screw-propeller and the angle of the diving planes. Lake boats, like today's submarines, submerged and surfaced while remaining level. Lake claimed that Holland's method made crewmen cling with the tenacity of barnacles as the boat submerged.

In 1897, Lake built *Argonaut,* the first submarine to operate successfully in the open sea. She was about 37 feet long, with two 10-foot-high, toothed, solid cast-iron wheels mounted under the hull, about 12 feet from the box. A smaller, pivoted wheel was mounted under the stern. Robert Burgess in

Lake went to Russia and built five submarines for the czarist navy. Russian sailors and dignitaries pose on the deck of this Lake-built submarine. At the time, she was the largest and most powerfully armed submarine in the world, carrying eight torpedo tubes. (Photo courtesy of the Submarine Force Library and Museum.)

One of two submarines Lake built for Austria. (Photo courtesy of the Submarine Force Library and Museum.)

Ships Beneath the Sea, wrote "These terrestrial appendages probably created more unfavorable feelings for the early Lake submarines than anything else he could have put on them. But he simply had a thing about putting wheels on underwater boats no matter how absurd some people thought they were. Even navy officers often asked him, 'What would happen if your submarine came to a precipice, Mr. Lake? Would it fall over the edge?' " Lake also invented submarine apparatus for locating and recovering sunken vessels and their cargoes. Like De Villeroi's *Alligator,* many of Lake's submarines included an air lock to allow a diver to leave the boat and explore the surrounding bottom or salvage a sunken vessel.

Lake had been unable to sell submarines to the U.S. Navy, but he had been busy elsewhere. The Russo-Japanese War led both belligerents to approach Lake. He sold Russia his 65-foot, 130-ton *Protector.* Then he and his technicians went to Russia to build five other boats for the Czarist navy. None of the Lake boats saw action in the war, but business was booming for the Lake Torpedo Boat Company.

Lake built Austria's first two submarines. In Germany he signed a contract with Krupp Works, and gave the armament company his design plans. Unfortunately, Lake failed to register his patents in Germany, and when Krupp built submarines he did so without paying royalties to Lake.

G-1

Simon Lake's first submarine for the U.S. Navy was laid down as *Seal* on February 2, 1909. The vessel was built by the Newport News Shipbuilding Company under a subcontract from the Lake Torpedo Boat Company. Margaret Lake, Simon's daughter, sponsored the new submarine at the launching in February 1911.

Above: G-1, *Simon Lake's first submarine for the U.S. Navy was launched in 1911.
Below: the submarine is shown with deck torpedo tube panels open. The tubes
were designed to be pivoted, giving the submarine the capability of firing torpedoes
broadside.* (Photos courtesy of the Submarine Force Library and Museum.)

Seal was unique because she was the first submarine built for the U.S.
Navy that was equipped with deck torpedo tubes, like those Lake had built
for Russia. When *Seal* was submerged the four tubes, two forward and two
aft, could be fired to either broadside. She also had two conventional bow
torpedo tubes in her hull. A diving chamber was installed between the two

tubes with a downward opening door through which a diver could leave the submarine. And Lake was not to be denied wheels on his latest creation, but for the first time they were retractable into the hull.

Seal was 161 feet long, with a beam of 13 feet 1 inch, and displaced 400 tons while surfaced and 540 tons when submerged. The submarine's two gasoline engines and twin screws produced almost 15 knots on the surface, while her electric motors could propel the boat at close to 11 knots submerged. *Seal* was equipped with a 10-ton drop keel that could be released by a quarter turn of a wrench for emergency ascent. She had a complement of 2 officers and 18 enlisted men.

During her acceptance trials she set diving and speed records for submarines of that era. A newspaper account of her record deep dive: "Diving steadily for 10 minutes into a 'hole' in Long Island Sound southwest of Bartlett's Reef lighthouse, the sub *Seal* reached a depth of 256 feet. . . Twelve men watched the indicators and by telephone they flashed the news to Navy officers and construction experts waiting at the surface."

The names of U.S. submarines were changed from the names of fishes and mammals to letters and numbers. Some claim it was because the secretary of the navy found it easier to deal with letters and numerals than with the names of marine life. *Seal* was renamed *G-1* in November 1911 and commissioned on October 28, 1912. Her designation was SS-*19 1/2*. No official explanation can be found for the "1/2," but *G-1* is the only submarine, and probably the only ship, ever to carry 1/2 in her official Navy designation.

G-1 joined the Atlantic Torpedo Flotilla for practice operations in Long Island Sound, Narragansett Bay, and Chesapeake Bay. During World War I, she served as a training ship for the newly established submarine base and submarine school at New London, Connecticut, an important role in preparing officers and men of the expanded submarine service that followed U.S. entry into the war. German U-boats were reported to be off the coast in June 1918, and *G-1* spent two four-day patrols in the vicinity of Nantucket, without incident. Her commander, Charles A. Lockwood, Jr., had graduated from the Naval Academy in 1912. He was the first high-ranking officer to realize during World War II that U.S. torpedoes were defective. He proved, with tests, that they ran too deep and their magnetic exploders did not always work (see Chapter 3). Lockwood later commanded the U.S. Pacific Fleet submarine force and eventually attained the rank of vice-admiral.

Lockwood wrote in *Down to the Sea in Subs,* "G-1 was an interesting boat, though totally unfit for service in a war such as the one in which we were engaged (World War I)." However, he stated, "Simon Lake was a man of imagination and vision, as shown by the retractable wheels on the *G-1*'s bottom and the diving chamber built between the two bow torpedo tubes."

The submarine was decommissioned on March 6, 1920, then was designated as a target for depth charge experiments. On June 21, 1921, the destroyer *Grebe* sank her with eight experimental depth charges. *G-1* settled to the bottom of Narragansett Bay in anchorage area A-3, 700 yards northeast of Taylor's Point, Rhode Island. The Navy failed in its effort to

▲ *Burt Mason, on the left, was responsible for salvaging many shipwrecks in the northeast. In 1962, he used a crane barge to salvage parts of* G-1. (Photo courtesy of Stewart Robinson.)

◀ *Crane lifts* G-1's *bow from 105 feet of water. Note the diving chamber's hatch to the right of the torpedo tube.* (Photo courtesy of Stewart Robinson.)

raise the submarine for additional depth charge experiments. The salvage report stated, "Have exhausted probability of raising G dash one with facilities available which consists of compressed air only. While vessel could probably be raised in due course by additional equipment, expense would be unwarranted. Board believes that even if raised some procedure would soon have to be repeated spending two weeks in salvage work before another explosion . . . allotment [of] one thousand dollars almost expended. Board recommends abandon salvage work and discontinue experiment. . . Board recommends efforts be made to sell G dash one to Salvage Company at scrap value. . ."

Diving *G-1*

The wreck, about 105 feet deep, was officially abandoned by the Navy on August 26, 1921, and sold for scrap the following year. However, not until the 1960s was she partially salvaged by professional salvors.

Burton H. Mason was a successful service manager of one of the largest fuel oil and equipment dealers in Connecticut. He was also a member of CUDA (Connecticut Underwater Diving Association). In January 1960, his only diving experience was to the bottom of a swimming pool. Mason later said, "a cup of coffee in a Bridgeport diner after a CUDA meeting cost me my job, my credit rating, and what had been heretofore a comparatively normal way of life." During the conversation, over coffee, one of the club members mentioned a German submarine sunk off Block Island. Mason left the diner with "dreams of ocean conquest, and a determination to locate the submarine in its watery grave."

Four months later, Mason had located and dived the German submarine, *U-853,* in about 130 feet of water. It was the first of many wrecks Mason would find and salvage. After diving the U-boat, he used a bank loan to buy a 40-foot salvage vessel. From then on, Mason focused on marine salvage, and little else.

He and two other divers found *G-1* in 1962 and raised much of the submarine for scrap. He removed her periscope, the first retractable one on a submarine, and converted it into a lamp. The submarine's depth gauge became a clock.

Today, scattered steel protrudes from a mud bottom. The curve of the pressure hull is apparent in many places. However, a diver attempting to follow the hull line in a circuit of the wreck will come upon areas that are completely devoid of wreckage. Strong current and very bad visibility make the dive hazardous. A good light and a strong tether line are strongly recommended. It is a very dark dive, and it is easy to lose contact with the wreck. There is so much boat traffic that it is dangerous to surface away from a dive boat. The Loran numbers are 14386.8 and 44010.7. Only a very experienced wreck diver should consider visiting *G-1*.

G-2

The second G-boat was also designed by Simon Lake. *G-2* (SS-*27*) was laid down in Bridgeport, Connecticut, as *Tuna* on April 21, 1909. But before she was launched by the Lake Torpedo Boat Company on January 10, 1912, her name was also changed to the less imaginative alpha-numeric designation.

The contract awarded to Lake was to pay $410,000 for the submarine, but stipulated that it must be completed within 28 months. The preliminary acceptance of *G-2* by the Navy was on November 7, 1913. Lake forfeited the contract and the submarine was completed at the New York (Brooklyn) Navy Yard, and commissioned February 6, 1915, Lieutenant (j.g.) Ralph C. Needham commanding. Technology had advanced so rapidly that by then *G-2*'s design had become obsolete. Her specifications were the same as *G-1*, except that she did not have the deck torpedo tubes.

Extensive modification and overhauling followed between March 26, 1916 and August 23, 1917. By that time the United States had entered World War I, but *G-2* had no combat encounters. She did perform defensive patrol duty off Block Island during July and August 1918, but her

Inside G-boat control room. Note the dive plane control wheels and the base of the periscope in the upper center. (Photo courtesy of the Submarine Force Library and Museum.)

G-boat's control room showing the submarine's helm. The ladder in front of the array of gauges leads up to the conning tower. (Photo courtesy of the Submarine Force Library and Museum.)

Forward torpedo room of a G-boat, showing the four torpedo tubes and their controls. (Photo courtesy of the Submarine Force Library and Museum.)

primary use was for training men at the New London Submarine School and experimental work on sound detection devices and magnetic detectors.

By the war's end *G-2* was considered unfit for military duty. She was decommissioned April 2, 1919, at New London, Connecticut, then she was designated for use as a target. A board was appointed to recommend procedures for conducting tests with depth charges to determine the effect of explosions on her hull and internal fittings while the submarine was submerged. *G-2* was moored in about 75 feet of water in Niantic Bay, near New London, with two mooring lines attached to straps around the vessel's

World War I submarine G-2 *served primarily for training and experiments. She sank at her anchorage in Niantic Bay, Connecticut on July 30, 1919 after serving as a depth charge target. Three men died in the disaster.* (Photo courtesy of the Submarine Force Library and Museum.)

G-2 *underway, circa 1916, with the submarine tender* Fulton (AS-1) *following astern.* (Photo courtesy of the Naval Historical Center.)

hull, about 25 feet from bow and stern, respectively. The mooring lines, which also acted as hauling down lines were led through rings on two 7,000-pound mushroom mooring anchors and to the stern of the Coast Guard cutter *Acushnet,* where they were made fast to bitts on the quarter deck. *Acushnet* was anchored with two anchors and lay about 200 yards from the submarine.

The submarine was submerged by trimming down as far as possible, allowing the crew to get out of the vessel, and secure the hatch from outside. *Acushnet* steamed ahead on her anchors and completely submerged the submarine by means of the hauling down lines. To aid in surfacing the boat, a salvage hose attached to a buoy for surface connections was connected to *G-2* for both ballast and compartment blowing.

Several experiments were conducted in Niantic Bay, Connectiuct, without any apparent serious damage. During her last test, the boat was submerged to 45 feet and a depth charge exploded 300 feet from the starboard beam. Then the boat was surfaced and examination revealed that the engine room hatch had been warped. The ballast tanks were blown dry, the hatch was removed, and it was sent to the New London Submarine Base to be straightened. The following morning, July 30, 1919, U.S. Navy Quartermaster First Class Clair E. Kirk, in charge of *G-2*, decided that, with the engine room hatch removed, it was necessary to float the stern as high out of the water as possible for safety reasons. He and a team of five men went below to blow the after ballast tanks.

Henry L. Wilkenson, of Pleasure Beach, Connecticut watched the submarine activity from his home. He noticed the stern slowly start to sink and realized that the boat was in trouble and men were aboard. He heard cries for help, then watched the bow suddenly rise as *G-2* slipped under the surface. The submarine sank in Two Tree Channel in Niantic Bay, near Pleasure Beach in about 75 feet of water trapping four of the work crew within the hull. Two men had managed to escape before the submarine went under.

The boat settled on an even keel. In shoulder deep water, within *G-2* Kirk worked his way to the conning tower. He did not panic; in pitch blackness, he found the handle to the conning tower hatch. When he opened the hatch, outrushing air propelled him to the surface, where he was rescued unconscious by crewmembers of *Acushnet*. His free ascent from the sunken submarine was the first within the U.S. Navy. One other man, Doyle Kervin, electrician 2nd class, who had been trapped inside, was rescued unconscious on the surface, but he died shortly after. Personnel at the submarine base said Kervin did not know how to swim. Two other men drowned.

After the tragedy, navy divers searched the submarine for the remaining two men but could not find them. Their bodies were later found floating in the bay.

A board of inquiry determined that *G-2* sank as a result of attempting to blow the after ballast tanks dry. Either the kingston valve (flood valve) was opened before sufficient air pressure had built up, causing water to back up into the blow system, or the vent valve was accidentally opened. As the stern sank, water rushed through the open engine room hatch, then into the forward hatch through which the men had entered the submarine, and the boat flooded rapidly. All hands were absolved of culpable negligence.

Because the Navy had planned to sink *G-2* with a depth charge after the tests, no attempt was made to salvage the boat. The submarine was stricken from the Navy list on September 11, 1919.

Salvage

During the Second World War, the U.S. War Production Board's special salvage projects section announced that a Boston salvage company had failed in an attempt to raise the submarine for scrap. In 1949, Clarence R. Edwards, an ex-Navy diver, with several other divers, salvaged the periscope, bronze sheathing around the conning tower, and some lead from the batteries. Edwards reported that some of the submarine's battery lead and her screw-propellers had been salvaged by others before him. However, sport divers in a 1961 magazine article reported that both screw-propellers were still attached to their shafts.

In 1951, a salvage boat was over the wreck site for several days, but suspended operations without removing any wreckage. In 1957, William McGuire and Company of New York City purchased salvage rights from the

A diver peers from one of G-2's *open hatches.* (Photo by Paul Tzimoulis.)

Paul Tzimoulis, aboard a dive-charter boat, holds his underwater camera. His left hand rests on one of G-2's bronze propeller hubs that he recovered. The 1,000-watt underwater lamp, beside the hub, was used for underwater photography. (Photo courtesy of the Submarine Force Library and Museum.)

Navy. The company's primary interest was the lead ballast. Members of a scuba diving club, the Connecticut Sea Devils, from Hartford, were given permission by the salvage company to dive *G-2*. Their two attempts to locate the submarine were unsuccessful, but when they returned a third time they found *G-2* buoyed. The *Hartford Times,* on August 12, 1957, reported "that the Navy, for the benefit of a national magazine, had placed a boiler buoy at either end of the sunken submarine." Apparently, the magazine wanted underwater photographs to accompany an article on the raising of *G-2*.

   The *West Hartford News* reported that one diver found the current "so rough you can't let go of the line and move around freely . . . the hull is so rusty there's nothing to hang onto." Another diver stated "It's amazing what you can do down there if you don't panic . . . I never worry, because if anything goes wrong I always have my Mae West there ready to inflate and carry me to the surface if I need it."

   The salvage company planned to raise the submarine by placing pontoons on the hull, sealing the hatches, and pumping air into the compartments. The company's hardhat divers found that *G-2* was on an even keel and not buried in the mud. A diver could walk under the bow and stern. The submarine, washed by the strong tidal current, was not covered with sediment. That should have made the salvage less difficult, but the attempt failed.

Diving *G-2*

G-2 was used as a training site for Navy divers and also became a very popular dive site. Sport divers from as far away as Florida and the Midwest visited the wreck and removed artifacts until 1962. Then a salvage company used a different approach to recovering the submarine. Submarine Specialists, Inc. of Hingham, Massachusetts blasted *G-2* with dynamite. Divers then hoisted her fragments into a bucket crane aboard a lighter.

Most of the submarine was recovered. What is left remains in Two Tree Channel off Seaside Park at Pleasure Beach, Connecticut, in about 75 feet of water. There are many rocks in the area, making it difficult to find the remaining pieces with a depth sounder. In a report of the accident to the chief of naval operations, the commander of the New London Submarine Base gave the bearings of the submarine as Goshen Point 84°, Two Tree Island 258°, and Millstone Point 289°. Another Navy report states *G-2* was midway between Magonk Point and Millstone Point, about a quarter mile offshore. The current is often strong (at times three to four knots), and dives should be made only at slack tide. Visibility is poor, and the few remains offer only slight prospects for finding artifacts.

Submarine Specialists, Inc. used explosives to salvage parts of G-2. *Two large pieces are shown, with a section of the stern on the right. Other salvors had attempted, without success, to raise the hull intact.* (Photo courtesy of the Submarine Force Library and Museum.)

CHAPTER 3

L-8—
Early Retiree

Location: south of Newport, Rhode Island
Approximate depth of water: 110 feet
Visibility: poor to bad
Current: little to moderate
Access: boat

A teenager impatiently waiting to be an adult looks on five years as an eternity. In the ageless universe, it scarcely rates as the blinking of an eye. It is neither of those to the United States Navy, but it is less than the Navy should expect from a costly, modern submarine, particularly one without enemy confrontation. That was the life span of *L-8* (SS-*48*), a victim of rapidly advancing technology that made her obsolete before her time.

In 1914, at the start of World War I, the U.S. Navy had 34 submarines, only 12 diesel-powered. That placed the country fourth in line behind France with 123, but mostly obsolete; Britain with 72, of which 17 were diesels; and Russia, with 42 submarines, 12 powered by diesels, some still undergoing shakedown.

Three years later, when the United States declared war on Germany, the L-class submarine was the latest advance in U.S. Navy development. They

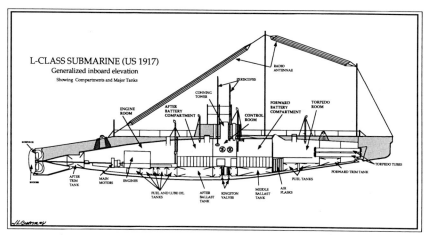

L-CLASS SUBMARINE (US 1917)
Generalized inboard elevation
Showing Compartments and Major Tanks

L-class submarine illustration by James L. Christley.

were armed with a three-inch deck gun, four bow torpedo tubes, and eight torpedoes. The deck guns were the first to be installed in United States submarines. They were inspired by the success of German U-boats early in the war, using deck guns to sink unarmed merchant ships. That conserved torpedoes and extended the length of their war cruises. The new deck guns were housed in a watertight well beneath the deck. They had to be raised before firing.

The Navy Department had been dependent upon private companies for design and construction of its submarines. It decided that L-class boats would be built at government yards as a first step in breaking that monopoly. Designs were submitted by Simon Lake, who had developed early Navy submarines and the Electric Boat Company, which had evolved from John Holland's Holland Boat Company.

The Electric Boat Company design was found to be superior, and required only one year to build, compared to two years for Lake's. However, the Electric Boat Company refused to release its designs for construction by the Navy. Therefore, Lake's was accepted, and *L-8* was built at the Navy's Portsmouth, New Hampshire, yard. For the O-class submarines that followed, the Electric Boat Company submitted to the Navy's demand and released its design plans to build the boats at government yards.

The new diesel powered *L-8* was designed to operate underwater at 10 1/2 knots. It could submerge to a depth of 200 feet, where the hull must withstand six times more pressure than at sea level. The submarine was 167 feet 4 inches long, displaced 456 tons surfaced, 524 tons submerged. She was constructed of steel, and carried a crew of two officers and 26 enlisted men. *L-8* was launched in April 1917, 47 days after the United States entered World War I. She was the first submarine off the ways at the Portsmouth Navy Yard, with hundreds more to follow.

The military fortunes of the entire U.S. Navy, including submarines, during World War I were strongly influenced by Plan Black, a contingency course of action that had been developed by naval strategies in the years prior to the war. It assumed that the powerful German battle fleet would head for United States waters or the Caribbean, battle the U.S. fleet, and if successful, invade the mainland. Information that the Germans were underway, would prompt the U.S. Navy to assemble for a gigantic mid-ocean confrontation. Pre-war naval exercises had concentrated on implementing Plan Black.

World War I

When war was declared, the Atlantic battle fleet was mobilized. Additional battleships, cruisers, destroyers, and patrol craft that had been decommissioned were ordered back into service to repel the U-boat assault that was expected along the eastern seaboard. Destroyers and submarines patrolled the coast, scouting for signs of the German fleet or the phantom hordes of U-boats, of which only six materialized.

While state-side admirals were implementing Plan Black, the U.S. Navy was represented in Britain by Admiral William C. Sims. He was the first to recognize that the U.S. Navy had prepared for the wrong kind of war. He was certain that there was no danger of the German Navy confronting the U.S. fleet, noting that the British had the Kaiser's navy securely bottled up in the North Sea. He also observed that the effectiveness of U-boats against merchant ships in European waters would keep them too occupied to launch extensive attacks against the United States mainland.

Sims warned that unless the marauding U-boats could be stopped quickly, losses of war material and troops would bring the Allies to their knees in a matter of months. He urged that Plan Black be scrapped. He asked that as many destroyers as possible be transferred to the European theater to conduct a concentrated hunt for U-boats, and that heavily guarded convoys be used to protect merchant ships from them. Only six destroyers were diverted to Europe in response to Admiral Sims' urgent plea. That token assistance did little to stem the loss of hundreds of tons of merchant shipping in British waters.

Naval authorities eventually recognized their error; there would be no great mid-Atlantic sea battle. Neither would there be swarms of U-boats in American waters, not while the approaches to Great Britain were so lucrative. Sims' recommendations were implemented. Naval strategy changed abruptly from emphasis on capital ships to building destroyers and

L-8 *in drydock.* (Photo courtesy of the National Archives.)

anti-submarine patrol craft. Additional destroyers were deployed to Europe to track down U-boats. Battleships were dispatched to the North Sea to keep the German fleet bottled up, and Britain was persuaded to adopt the convoy system.

Although *L-8* was launched very early in the war, and her armament was formidable, she never engaged in a war action, nor did any American submarine play a major role in the war. One L-class boat did manage to survive a unique experience at a net loss of one U-boat for the Germans. She was straddled by two U-boats, one fired a torpedo at her and missed. It hit and sank the second U-boat.

Decoy Tactics

On October 25, 1918, *L-8* was assigned one of the war's most unusual roles. As early as 1915, the British had deployed decoy trawlers, harmless in themselves but towing a submerged submarine instead of fishing nets. An unsuspecting U-boat might be duped into a surface attack on such an apparently defenseless target. The submarine would then slip her tow to

L-8 *iced in with* G-2. *Both submarines were designed by Simon Lake and both would be expended as test targets.* (Photo courtesy of the Submarine Library and Museum.)

attack the U-boat with torpedoes. The ruse was initially successful; two U-boats, *U-40* and *U-23,* were destroyed by the tactic. Unfortunately, when *U-23* was sunk, her survivors were allowed to mingle with several interned German civilians to whom they described the deception. When the civilians were repatriated, that information was relayed to German naval authorities. From then on, U-boat captains were on the alert against such tactics.

The U.S. Navy decided to try the trawler-towed submarine approach in American waters during 1918. A four-masted schooner, *Charles Whittemore,* served as a tow for the submarine *N-5.* The two worked out of Block Island, Rhode Island, patrolling the offshore shipping lanes during August and September, with no U-boat encounters. The schooner was then ordered to Charleston, South Carolina, to take *L-8* in tow for patrol in the Azores. It was not a very exciting prospect for the submarine crew, but it might afford an opportunity to test *L-8*'s 3-inch deck gun and her four torpedo tubes against the enemy. That opportunity never materialized, however, because when the towed submarine, en route to the Azores, reached Bermuda on November 13, 1918, it was two days after the end of the war.

For two years after the war, *L-8* served with a flotilla assigned to China. By 1922, only five years after her launching, the L-class submarine was obsolete. She was by then attached to the West Coast Submarine Flotilla at

San Pedro, California. She left San Pedro on July 25 and arrived at Hampton Roads, Virginia on September 28 in what seems to have been a leisurely two-month cruise. Whether or not by intent, it delayed the inevitable until November 15, 1922, when she was decommissioned. Two years later, she was at the Philadelphia Navy Yard, waiting to be stripped before disposal. Side by side with her were three of her sister boats, *L-5, L-6,* and *L-7.*

Weapon Test

During the war, 28 Allied capital ships, consisting of battleships and cruisers, had been sunk by German U-boats. That demonstrated a vulnerability that compelled world-wide naval designers to increase the armor plating of large warships for better protection against torpedo attack. In turn, a search was launched for more destructive weaponry. In the United States, the Newport Naval Torpedo Station developed an exotic solution: a magnetic-influence exploder that would sense disturbance of the Earth's magnetic field as a metal-hulled ship moved through the water. The exploder was designed to fire a charge in the warhead of a torpedo as it passed through that disturbance, under the relatively unprotected lower hull of an armor-plated ship. The resulting blast was calculated to break the back of even a massive battleship.

The development was ready for live testing by February 1924, but the Navy refused to provide a battleship for use as a target. By January 1925, the compelling need to prove the worth of the revolutionary development forced the designers to scale down their request to a more modest target— an obsolete submarine hulk. The Navy finally agreed to provide one of the four L-class submarines that were being stripped at Philadelphia. *L-8* was chosen as the most seaworthy, although she had to be towed to Newport for the test.

On May 26, 1926, the first of two torpedoes equipped with the new exploder was fired at the submarine; it passed harmlessly underneath, a sad omen of how ineffectual it would prove to be in the early days of World War II, but unfortunately, an omen that was ignored. The second torpedo did explode in an impressive column of gas and water that sent *L-8* to the bottom, and reassured supporters of the project.

Weapon Failure

The commander of the Newport Torpedo Station, Captain Thomas Hart, referred to the exploder test in a letter to the chief of ordnance as, "the opening of a new phase of torpedo warfare which gives the United States a tremendous advantage over any prospective enemy." Hart's unfounded claim

Above: A torpedo equipped with a magnetic-influence exploder passing harmlessly under L-8 in tests off Newport, Rhode Island. This failure should have alerted the Navy to the ineffectiveness of the new device. Below: L-8 was sunk on the second try, the only destructive test in 19 years of pre-World War II development and production of magnetic-influence exploders. (Photos courtesy of the Naval Historical Center.)

was anything but prophetic. Its irony would not be evident until the first two years of World War II, when U.S. torpedoes equipped with the same magnetic influence exploders were totally ineffective against the Japanese. They ran too deep, and their highly touted exploders fired either prematurely or not at all. Those deficiencies were never revealed before the war because *L-8* was the only destructive test conducted during the 19 years of pre-World War II magnetic exploder development, production, and stockpiling.

In 1943, magnetic-influence exploder devices were discredited and discarded—not only by the United States, but also by the British and Germans. During World War II, American submarines accounted for 1,314 Japanese naval and merchant ships sunk, for a total of 5.3 million tons, or 55% of the enemy losses. That impressive toll might have been achieved during the first two years of the war if U.S. submarines had been equipped with more efficient torpedoes.

No one can assess the extent to which the war might have been shortened, how many costly invasions such as Iwo Jima and Okinawa might have been avoided—nor whether atomic bombs would have dropped on Hiroshima and Nagasaki if American torpedoes had been more reliable early in the war.

For more than 50 years, the hulk of *L-8* lay in obscurity, 110 feet below the surface, 5,520 yards from Brenton Reef Light, off the coast of Newport. Obsolete and expendable, without a notable war record, her remains were soon forgotten. But one glory was hers, alone. *L-8* was the first U.S. Navy submarine off the ways at the Portsmouth Navy Yard, first of the many that were to follow.

Diving *L-8*

During the summer of 1980 an enterprising scuba diver from Connecticut, Mike Gormotsky, was attracted to two wreck symbols shown on a NOAA nautical chart of the area south of Newport. With his own boat, using Loran-C and a graph recording depth sounder, Gormotsky and several friends, launched a search for the wrecks. Search patterns drawn on the chart and lots of luck rewarded their efforts with a promising outline on the bottom after only 30 minutes. An anchor was grappled into the wreck and one of the divers, Dan Riley, dove to determine if their find was a wreck or an outcropping of rock.

Riley confirmed that they had locked onto a small steel hull. Gormotsky then dove. When he surfaced, he not only confirmed Riley's finding; he identified the prize as what appeared to be a submarine—U.S. Navy submarine *L-8* had been located.

The wreck site is well known. It is in 110 feet of water, and the Loran coordinates are 14423.04, 25776.0, and 43959.0. There is no appreciable current to add hazard to the dive. However, visibility is almost always bad—usually only 5-10 feet; 15 feet is highly unusual. The condition is created by the outflow of sediment from Narragansett Bay and Long Island Sound. It clouds a diver's vision just before the wreck is reached. The conditions worsen as divers swim around the submarine, stirring up the silt that overlays everything in the area.

Exploration reveals *L-8* listing 20° to port. Considering that the submarine was sunk by a torpedo, the pressure hull is remarkably more intact than one would expect. The exterior of the conning tower and other streamlining exteriors, however, are badly decomposed.

Several compartment hatches are open, inviting penetration of the submarine's interior. The forward torpedo room is accessible through the torpedo loading hatch and a very large damage hole. A diver entering through the damage hole is forward in the room. The four 900-lb solid brass torpedo tubes were recovered by sport divers during the winter of 1990-1991.

The bottom of the interior is covered with two feet of sediment that is stirred up by even the most cautious diver,—reducing the poor visibility to zero visibility. Photographs must be taken ahead of a diver. All that has been passed on the way in is obscured by a dense cloud of sediment. The condition can be controlled to some degree by removing fins before penetration to reduce disturbance of the water.

On one of his charters to *L-8*, Captain Bill Palmer of the dive-charter boat *Thunderfish* penetrated to the engine room, where he removed a small telegraph unit mounted to the ceiling.

A project was launched in July 1989, to remove the submarine's last screw-propeller. Steve Moy and several divers from the Aquidneck Island Diving shop in Newport, Rhode Island, ran a dive charter to *L-8*. After viewing the port side screw-propeller, they decided that it would be feasible to make an attempt to remove it. Several weeks later, another group of divers stopped by the scuba shop and stated that they intended to remove the same screw-propeller and sell it for scrap.

Don Gunning, who runs the dive shop, had heard of how the starboard screw-propeller had been removed years before and sold for its metal value. He declared to the authors, "It was a shame and a waste. No one got to see it and learn of the history of the submarine." Gunning and several friends decided that the remaining screw-propeller should be recovered and put on display. The vast majority of Rhode Island residents were not aware that *L-8* lay off their coast. If the artifact could be recovered, they would have the opportunity to view it, and be introduced to *L-8*'s history.

Above: L-8's port screw-propeller. The artifact generated a salvage race between groups of divers to prevent it from being sold for scrap. (Photo by Brian Skerry.) *Below:* The same screw-propeller on board the salvage vessel after it was recovered by (left to right) Donald Gunning, Stephen Moy, Eva Longobardi, Kenny Sheehan, Greg DeAscentis and Mark Frelond. The successful recovery of the relic by this group assured its preservation. (Photo by Don Gunning.)

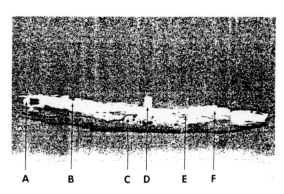

A side-scan sonar printout of L-8 after more than half a century on the bottom reveals the rudder and rudder supports (A); personnel hatch (B); remains of the conning tower's streamlining (C); the conning tower (D); the gun mount and personnel hatch area (E); and the torpedo hatch (F). (Courtesy of American Underwater Search and Survey, Ltd.)

This 900-lb solid bronze torpedo tube was recovered from L-8 in November 1990 by Bill Palmer and donated to the Submarine Force Library and Museum at Groton, Connecticut.

Gunning vowed that the relic would be preserved. He assembled a dive team and chartered a local fishing vessel. It took two days of diving to recover the 1,372-pound bronze screw-propeller. An acetylene torch was used to burn through the prop-shaft, a more difficult task than expected because it was composed of two alloys, monel surrounded by bronze.

Gunning, who teaches commercial as well as sport diving, told the authors, "We used the experience we have gained through the commercial diving industry to go out and perform the operation. We do not recommend that the average diver go out and attempt a similar project. We have to knock on wood, but there were no accidents, no problems, and the operation came off as we planned it." He also informed us that they "did not do this out of greed, or to be the first to do it, or to just get the prop. We did it so that someone else would not take it and sell it for its metal value."

The screw-propeller is now on display in front of Gunning's Aquidneck Island Diving shop, Newport, Rhode Island.

Brass valve handles inscribed with information such as the manufacturer's name and other artifacts of brass or bronze have been recovered, providing treasured mementos for visiting sports divers to cherish—lasting memories of their brief dive into history.

CHAPTER 4

S-5—
Test Dive Victim

Location: over 40 miles off the Delaware Capes
Approximate depth of water: 170 feet
Visibility: excellent
Current: little to moderate
Access: boat

President Woodrow Wilson faced the dismal prospect of war for the United States as early as the first year of World War I, although military action was confined to Europe and the seas around Europe. Despite ample evidence of America's pro-Allied preference, as a neutral she was spared from action. It was difficult to maintain that status while the volume of war supplies flowing across the Atlantic to Britain and her allies was developing into a deciding factor in the war. Vessels of the United States sailing the war zone waters were certain to draw the country into the conflict unless an effective deterrent could be found.

Wilson, like other presidents before and after him, was certain that the only way to avoid war was to arm the country so heavily that no nation would dare to attack her. He asked the Navy's General Board for recommendations. No one should have been surprised at the advice that group of senior admirals offered—a building program to provide a navy "ultimately equal to the most powerful maintained by any nation in the world." Their 1915 report specified that the objective should be achieved by building battleships, cruisers, destroyers—and submarines.

The naval appropriation approved by Congress included funds to add approximately 100 submarines to the Navy. Three new classes, designated O, R, and S, would be built in addition to several experimental models. The first two, O and R, were slightly improved versions of the last of the L-class boats (*L-9* through *L-11*) that had been designed earlier for coastal defense. There was no change in the 167-foot length, submerged displacement of 548 tons, 4 torpedo tubes, and 8 torpedoes. Forty-three of those enhanced models were built.

The S-class program introduced a new bidding process in which decisions were made by the Navy. The design of earlier submarines had been left to the discretion of the builder as long as Navy specifications were satisfied. The contract to build *S-1* was awarded to Electric Boat Company, successor after 1904 to the submarine pioneering Holland Boat Company. The Lake Torpedo Boat Company was granted the order for *S-2* and *S-3*. The first submarine to be designed by the U.S. Navy would be built at the Portsmouth Navy Yard.

Lake's *S-2* was unacceptable and was dropped from the program. The Busch-Sulzer diesel engines in *S-2* had considerably more horsepower than the New London Ship & Engine Company diesel engines in *S-1* and *S-3*. Lake had gambled that his prototype would be faster than the other two models. On the first test for the Navy Department's Board of Inspection and Survey one of *S-2*'s engines dropped a valve. After repairs the test was rescheduled, but both main engines burned out and it required four months to repair them.

Lake's gamble failed and the Navy design was adopted for *S-4* to *S-17*; and Electric Boat's design was used on *S-18* to *S-41*. New performance requirements were added for extended range and greater endurance, establishing the need for bigger hulls and larger engines. A second Electric Boat design was adopted for *S-42* to *S-47* and a new Navy design was applied to *S-48* to *S-51*. Some of the Navy design boats were assigned to the Lake Torpedo Boat Company under construction contract.

The new S-class submarines reflected a notable advance over earlier models. They ranged from 219 to 265 feet in length, with submerged displacement of 1,062 to 1,230 tons, and carried from 12 to 16 torpedoes. Before the construction program was completed, eight were even equipped with a stern torpedo tube, the first in the history of the U.S. Navy. *S-1* achieved a unique distinction as the U.S. Navy's only aircraft-carrying submarine. She carried an XS-1 floatplane which could be dismantled and stowed in a cylindrical container on her stern.

"S-boat Sinks," became a familiar headline between the world wars. S-5 *was the first to receive that recognition.* (Photo courtesy of the Naval Historical Center.)

By 1925, all 51 were completed; however, "S-boat Sinks" became a familiar headline between the world wars. By 1927, 6 had gone down, with 73 men lost. The first was *S-5* in 1920, followed by *S-48* in 1921, then *S-36* and *S-39* in 1923, all without loss of life. Two years later, *S-51* was rammed by a steamer off Block Island, Rhode Island, and 33 of her 36 man crew perished. In 1927, *S-4* was rammed by the Coast Guard cutter *Paulding* off Provincetown, Massachusetts, with the loss of all 40 of her crew.

S-5 (SS-*110*) was commissioned on March 6, 1920. After completion of sea trials she was assigned early in August to participate in the Maine Centennial celebration. In mid-August she was ordered on a recruiting mission, a tour that would include Baltimore, Washington, Richmond, Savannah and Bermuda. As the new submarine left Boston on August 30, she passed a sooty, once-white, ancient freighter, *Alanthus*. That cargo ship was to affect the lives of every member of *S-5*'s crew within a few days.

Sea tests were conducted and all systems were working well as the submarine headed for Baltimore. A speed run on the morning of September 1 was followed by a five-hour submerged run. At about 2 p.m. that afternoon, Lieutenant Commander Charles M. Cooke, Jr., in command of *S-5*, ordered a crash dive test. The submarine was 54 miles southeast of Cape Henlopen, Delaware, far enough offshore to be out of the heavily traveled shipping lanes. Diving and surfacing tests could be carried out in that area without concern for sea traffic.

The emergency dive was specified to be completed within one minute to reduce exposure to attack by surface vessels or aircraft. The test is a routine training procedure, one that had been successfully performed by *S-5* the day before. Commander Cooke sounded the diving alarm. On conditioned response, ballast tanks were flooded and the hydroplanes were properly angled for submerging.

The Sinking

S-5 responded to the descent with more than usual speed. As the submarine submerged, seawater poured through the ventilation system into the control room, engine room, torpedo room, and the electric motor room. Normal practice was to leave the air intake valve open until the diesel engines came to a full stop, just before completely submerging. That would conserve air for the crew, but the timing was so critical that the responsibility was assigned to the boat's chief noncommissioned officer. In this case, Chief Gunners' Mate Percy Fox was responsible for pulling a lever to close the valve. He was momentarily distracted and when water began to pour out of the ventilators he yanked the lever—but the valve jammed in the open position.

Water continued to flood each of the main compartments through the air induction system until, one by one, their control valves were closed by the crew. One exception, the forward torpedo room valve, refused to budge and the crew was forced to abandon the compartment, securing the watertight bulkhead hatch behind them.

Commander Cooke tried to bring the submarine back to the surface while his crew endeavored to stem the inrushing sea. Despite their efforts, *S-5* continued her descent, even with forward and middle ballast tanks blown and hydroplanes at "hard rise." The flooded torpedo room and 80 tons of water in the bilges carried the submarine bow first into the muddy bottom. As *S-5* came to rest, her conning tower depth gauge read 170 feet.

Nothing could be done to eject the water in the forward torpedo room, but an effort was launched to empty the bilges. The heavy demand was more than the bilge pump could take. When it blew a gasket and could not be repaired, the 37-man crew and four officers knew they were in real trouble. Escape lungs were unknown in U.S. Navy submarines, although Germany had developed a crude version during World War I. *U-59* was equipped with that life-saving device when it was sunk late in the war, off the British coast in 100 feet of water. Several of her crew reached the surface alive, but without using their escape lungs. If they had been saved by them, the attendant publicity might have prompted their acceptance by the United States for S-class boats.

S-5 was at almost twice the depth of Germany's *U-59*—without escape lungs and no chance of survival in free escape. There was no possibility of surfacing the bow-heavy submarine and her crew from the bottom. They were operating outside heavily travelled sea lanes, and no one knew of the sinking.

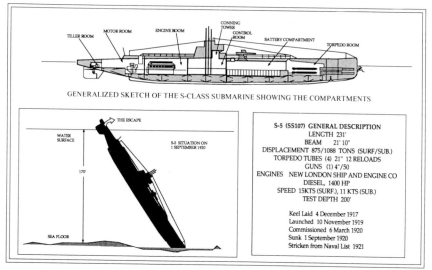

GENERALIZED SKETCH OF THE S-CLASS SUBMARINE SHOWING THE COMPARTMENTS

WATER
SURFACE

THE ESCAPE

S-5 SITUATION ON
1 SEPTEMBER 1920

170'

SEA FLOOR

S-5 (SS107) GENERAL DESCRIPTION
LENGTH 231'
BEAM   21' 10"
DISPLACEMENT 875/1088 TONS (SURF/SUB.)
TORPEDO TUBES (4) 21" 12 RELOADS
GUNS (1) 4"/50
ENGINES NEW LONDON SHIP AND ENGINE CO
DIESEL, 1400 HP
SPEED 15KTS (SURF.), 11 KTS (SUB.)
TEST DEPTH 200'

Keel Laid 4 December 1917
Launched 10 November 1919
Commissioned 6 March 1920
Sunk 1 September 1920
Stricken from Naval List 1921

Commander Cooke's escape plan involved floating the aft section of S-5 *so the stern would rise above the water.* (Illustration by James L. Christley.)

Escape Plan

Almost certain death confronted the crew, until Commander Cooke was inspired with an ingenious escape plan. He reasoned that, with the depth gauge reading 170 feet, it might be possible to raise the stern of the 231-foot long submarine high enough for it to extend above the surface. He knew that if sufficient buoyancy was applied to the aft section, the stern would rise. As the stern moved upward, the water in the motor, engine and control rooms would drain forward into the battery room, further increasing the stern's buoyancy.

The plan had some serious risk because shifting the water into the battery room would allow seawater to mix with the sulphuric acid of the batteries. That would generate deadly chlorine gas. The watertight doors to the battery room would have to be closed as soon as water had drained in and before the gas could reach a dangerous level. Cooke knew the magnitude of the risk he was taking. But, he and his crew were lost unless he took that chance—and won.

Cooke's plan was put into action. He ordered the aft ballast tanks blown; the submarine shuddered, but remained stuck to the muddy bottom. Then, precious air was blown into the aft diesel tanks to replace the fuel that was now useless. The stern responded, slowly lifting off the bottom. Water spilled over the door sills flowing forward from one compartment to the

S-5's stern extends above water with her crew trapped inside. (Photo courtesy of the Naval Historical Center.)

next. Suddenly, the stern shot to the surface as tons of seawater cascaded forward carrying men, floor plates, and loose equipment along with it. Crewmen were washed from one compartment to another, several into the battery room where they had to swim to stay afloat. One struck his head against the bulkhead and would have drowned except for the assistance of others who kept him afloat.

The stern rose until the submarine was almost vertical. That made the door, high over the heads of the swimming men, inaccessible to them. Ensign John Longstaff in the next compartment, the ward room, fashioned a rope out of curtains. He lowered it into the battery room and pulled the men to safety. The watertight door to the battery room was then secured.

By that time chlorine gas had escaped into the ward room, forcing the men farther astern to the control room. The persistent fumes seeped into that compartment, and gas masks were donned by all but three crewmen. It was imperative to move men without masks further aft. That proved to be no easy task. The next compartment was the engine room, and the door to it had slammed closed as seawater rushed forward during the ascent of S-5's stern. Because of the submarine's inclination, the door was higher than the heads of the men below, and it was under 3 or 4 feet of water.

It was impossible to open the closed door from below. Fortunately, the communication system was still operating; the men below called the engine room for assistance. The door was forced open by pushing from underneath and pulling from above. As it opened, tons of water poured down on those below. With rescue in sight, they managed to climb hand over hand into the engine room and secure the watertight door behind them. The dimming lights held up long enough to illuminate the scene while the task was being completed.

The entire 37-man crew crowded into the three aft compartments, engine room, electric motor room, and small tiller room at the extreme stern. The welcome sound of water lapping against the hull was proof that at least part of the submarine was above the surface. It was determined by tapping that about 17 feet of the stern projected above water.

The air supply in an S-class submarine would normally keep her crew alive for about 72 hours, but most of *S-5*'s compartments were flooded or sealed. Something needed doing, quickly. Several hours after the sinking, Commander Cooke decided to try to force a hole through the submarine's 3/4-inch steel hull. The tiller room was selected as the best location because it was the farthest astern.

S-5 was not equipped with the heavy tools that were needed to break through the thick steel hull. The first attempts were made with a small hand drill. Pressure and patience finally wore a small hole, about the diameter of a wooden pencil, through to the outside. Although tapping had indicated that the stern was above water, the crew was reassured when no water poured through the tiny opening. With part of the submarine projecting out of the water, there was some prospect of rescue by a passing ship, even out of the heavily travelled sea routes. But so far, there was no way the small hole could contribute to such a rescue.

The crew resumed work with the hand drill, but the task went slowly. Then, an electric drill with a 3/8-inch bit was found in the engine room and put to use. It was much more effective, but those who used it paid a painful penalty. Those power circuits that were still operating were badly grounded and what clothing the men wore was soaking wet. When the drill was turned on, the body of the man operating it became an electrical conductor to ground, knotting his muscles and gripping his entire body with pain. The men suffered the punishment by providing frequent relief for the drill operator. A little more of the steel barrier between them and freedom was removed. Then, electrical power failed completely, leaving the interior in total darkness. Later the crew claimed that the dark, even more than foul air, was the most difficult strain they had to contend with. The ordeal seemed endless.

A group of four holes had been drilled through the hull before the power failure. The metal between those holes was removed by laboring all night with hack saw blades. By daylight, a two square-inch opening, measuring one-half by four inches, had been drilled and sawed to the outside world. As Commander Cooke peered through, he helplessly watched a ship pass less than five miles away. He withheld that discouraging information from the crew. Instead, he concentrated on some means to attract the attention of any other vessels that might pass by.

As work on enlarging the hole continued with the hand drill two more ships passed, too far off to see the submarine, or if they did, they would have taken it for no more than floating debris. The crew had expected that the opening would provide circulation of fresh air into the submarine, but it did not. The volume of carbon dioxide exhaled by 37 men was more than the fresh air flow capacity of the small hole.

Work on enlarging the opening continued. The men who were drilling and cutting had to be relieved after only two minute periods because of the foul air. By 2 p.m., 24 hours after the sinking, the hole had been enlarged to a 12 square-inch triangle, measuring about four by six inches. By then, the bit of the drill was almost useless, and further efforts to enlarge the opening were abandoned. Instead, an undershirt, fastened to a 10-foot length of pipe was extended through the hole, and was continuously waved to attract attention.

Throughout the travail of S-5's crew, the ancient cargo ship that they had passed as they left Boston, had lumbered along the same route the submarine had taken. The dingy old vessel, S.S. *Alanthus,* on her way to be scrapped, came into view at about 3 p.m. First, she seemed to respond to the waving signal with a change of direction toward the submarine. Then, she suddenly changed course, and passed out of view of the distraught submariners. Later, Commander Cooke remarked, "I think that was the most terrible moment the crew suffered. They were congratulating themselves on their discovery, and to have the ship turn and leave them to their fate was almost more than they could bear."

Rescue

As *Alanthus* left the scene, her captain pondered on what had attracted his attention. He realized that it might have been more than driftwood, perhaps a distress signal. He turned back, with anticipation mounting as his ship approached the strange sight; then he sent a boat alongside the upended S-5.

Jubilation was unbounded aboard the submarine. Rescue was at hand after all had seemed lost. Cables were looped around the stern of the submarine to ensure that she would not go under again. A small water pump was improvised to force air in to the oxygen-starved crew, and buckets of freshwater were poured into a funnel through the opening to the imprisoned men who had been without food or water for hours in a temperature of more than 120 degrees.

Alanthus could do no more without assistance. She had no cutting tools to free the trapped crew, but she could radio a distress signal. That is, she would have been able to radio a call for help except that her only radioman had been left behind at Boston. Instead, distress flags were flown to attract the attention of any passing ship. At about 6:20 p.m. the northbound Pan-American Line steamer *George W. Goethals* sighted the distress signal and headed to it at full speed. She put a boat over the side, and the chief

The old freighter Alanthus *standing by* S-5*'s stern after sighting the stricken submarine.* (Photo courtesy of the Naval Historical Center.)

officer, the radio operator, two doctors and the chief engineer came along-side the sunken *S-5* for consultation.

Goethals was without the kind of cutting equipment that was needed to free the submarine crew, but she did have an operating radio that sent out a message to the U.S. Navy, calling for help. The call was picked up by a ham operator in Connecticut, then relayed to the Navy. The Navy dispatched a rescue team, the battleship *Ohio* at sea, two destroyers from the Norfolk Navy Base, one from New York, and another from Philadelphia, in addition to a salvage vessel from the Brooklyn Navy Yard.

William G. Grace, the liner's chief engineer, decided not to wait for the Navy, if the men were to be saved. He, with occasional relief from his assistant, used what tools they had to enlarge the opening in the hull of the submarine. They worked with drills, ratchets, hacksaws, and a crowbar. By 10 p.m., the hole measured ten inches by 12 inches, and by midnight it was increased to a diameter of 20 inches. It was 1:45 a.m., after seven hours' work, before the hole was large enough for a man to pass through. The survivors were moved out, first the unconscious, then the injured. It took a full hour to evacuate all the men because they were so weakened by their ordeal. Commander Cooke, the last to leave, secured the watertight door into the motor room before he left. It was 3:34 a.m. September 3, 1920, more than 37 hours after *S-5* plunged to the bottom.

The ordeal had left the submarine crew exhausted, but with no serious injuries. The three who had been exposed to chlorine gas without gas masks were later treated at the Philadelphia Navy Yard hospital. The exemplary conduct of the crew throughout the crisis reflected the highest credit on the men, their officers, and the Navy. Each emergency had been confronted without complaint, with the men carrying out orders to the limits of their physical endurance.

Salvage Effort

The first naval vessels to arrive after the rescue included the battleship *Ohio,* the salvage vessel *Mallard,* and the destroyer *Biddle.* The latter carried all survivors except Commander Cooke to the Philadelphia Navy Yard. Cooke stayed behind aboard *Ohio* to oversee the efforts to salvage his command. The high spirits of the rescued crew were reflected by one of the men who raised his voice in a comic rendition of "How Dry I Am" as he walked down the gangplank in Philadelphia.

En route to Philadelphia, the men signed a letter to the secretary of the navy, extolling Commander Cooke. They asked that they be allowed to serve under him again after *S-5* was salvaged. Lt. Commander Cooke eventually attained the rank of Admiral, serving as chief of staff to Admiral Ernest J. King in World War II. Ensign Longstaffe, who had rescued the men from the battery room, attained the rank of captain. He directed a squadron of submarines in the Pacific that wreaked havoc on World War II Japanese shipping.

Back at the scene of the sinking, *Ohio* secured the stern of the submarine with a 6-inch towing cable to drag her into shallow water. During the slow journey a storm blew up, and after only three and one-half miles of towing heavy seas parted the cable. *S-5* bobbed only once before she again plunged to the bottom, this time forever.

Buoys marked the location for the Navy salvage vessels *Mallard* and *Beaver.* Divers reported *S-5* to be in 144 feet of water on a hard, sandy bottom on her port side with her bow pointing east. The surface-tended divers encountered storms and strong currents that hampered their salvage attempts, until the Navy ordered discontinuance of the operation on November 19, 1920.

The salvage vessel *Falcon* resumed efforts on May 3, 1921 with 25 divers working steadily for almost four months. They found the submarine listing about 20° to port and down by the bow about six feet. After 477 dives, an attempt to raise *S-5* failed due to air leaks that made it impossible to blow the flooded compartments clear of water. The persistent interference of storms impeded all efforts to attach pontoons for flotation. The salvage was abandoned, and on August 29 the submarine was struck from the Navy list.

Diving *S-5*

More than 60 years later, Milt Herschenriter, captain of the dive boat *Matusalan,* out of Stone Harbor, New Jersey, launched an extensive search for the submarine. He, his wife Suzanna, Joe Milligan, Stephen Sokolosf, George Hughes, and Kelly Rawley devoted two and a half years to the project. They used a nautical chart marked with the Navy's reported position for *S-5*. During one of their searches in 1985, they assisted a lobsterman who was trying to retrieve his trapped gear. The appreciative lobsterman provided the Loran-C numbers of a shipwreck where some of his pots had become entangled. The location (38°-41′ N, 74°-08′ W) was one mile north of *S-5*'s plotted position on the nautical chart. Based on the available charts, it was too far off to be the submarine, but it seemed to be a previously undiscovered wreck, and that was an exciting prospect for any avid wreck diver.

Navy salvage reports state that the submarine is in 144 feet of water. When the dive boat reached the wreck site, her depth recorder read 170 feet, further indication that it could not be *S-5*. Joe Milligan recalls his first dive at the scene: "We had no idea what to expect. When the wreck came up on the depth recorder, it looked just like a spike. Since this was not the reported position for *S-5,* and the depth was deeper than stated, we expected to be diving on an old barge or some less interesting wreck. As soon as I reached 50 or 60 feet, however, I could see a submarine lying on the bottom in an upright position, with a list of 15° to 20°, to the portside. It was fantastic—pure elation—a really beautiful dive."

Visibility is excellent because the wreck is so far offshore—more than 40 miles. Milligan has reported that visibility on every dive has been between 50 and 100 feet. He portrays the entire wreck as a highly visible panorama with lobsters all over—15 and 16 pounders. A hard hat divers' platform, left over from the Navy's 1921 salvage effort, is off the portside stern. Like other sunken submarines on the eastern seaboard, *S-5*'s pressure hull is intact, but most of the outer plating has oxidized and disappeared. In addition, like many other wrecks, her hull is draped with a trawler's net. At least one fishing captain has blasphemed the submarine's remains.

All hatches are open, providing ease of entry into the wreck. The conning tower hatch cover had been replaced with a steel plate and a rubber gasket was bolted into place to make the compartment air tight for flotation. When Milligan and his divers removed that plate, they found the conning tower free of sediment. Elsewhere, 60 years had accumulated one to three feet of silt through the open hatches.

Depth to the deck is 160 feet, limiting down time and requiring decompression depending on the length of the dive. Therefore, scuba divers must operate efficiently in the best possible visibility. Captain Herschenriter allows each diver to select a specific compartment to dive without interference. That prevents loss of visibility from sediment stirred up by another diver.

The bow area is like a large sieve, open to the sea. During the Navy's salvage attempt, S-5 was dragged toward shore with her bow scraping the bottom, apparently damaging the underside. Light penetrates under the deck plates into the forward torpedo room. Navy salvage reports mention that when they tried to pump air into the submarine, a tremendous amount escaped from that compartment.

The naval career of S-5 was short and uneventful except for the dramatic rescue of her entire crew. She remains today, an historic memorial to the loss of a new submarine through human error—and an equally historic testimony to the survival of her entire crew by the application of man's intelligence, ingenuity, and determination.

Salvage vessel Mallard *alongside S-5's stern with the battleship* Ohio *in the background. The submarine was later lost when a cable parted while* Ohio *had her under tow.* (Photo courtesy of the Naval Historical Center.)

================= **CHAPTER 5** =================

S-16 and *S-21—*
Two Targets

S-16
Location: 18 miles southwest of Key West, Florida
Approximate depth of water: 250 feet
Visibility: excellent
Current: little to extreme
Access: boat

S-21
Location: about three miles southeast of Halfway Rock, Casco Bay, Maine
Approximate depth of water: 160 feet
Visibility: poor to good
Current: little to moderate
Access: boat

Most navies considered the submarine a coastal defense weapon before World War I. However, during that "Great War," Germany produced a weapon that could strike the enemy without warning. U-boats accounted for the destruction of 5,708 Allied ships totaling an incredible 11,018,655 tons. In addition to merchant shipping, 28 Allied capital ships (battleships and cruisers) were sunk. A few U-boats had forced the most powerful navy in the world, the British Grand Fleet, to retreat from its unprotected anchorage at Scapa Flow. Of even more importance, it drove the British from the main theater of naval action—the North Sea.

During the war, the U.S. Navy recognized the offensive potential of underwater warships. New American submarine programs were for longer-range vessels that incorporated all the lessons learned from the war. The S-class submarines were a product of the new development program, but were incapable of long, aggressive war patrols. The missions of S-boats were limited to about thirty days, not by a shortage of fuel, food, or water, but more by a crew's ability to endure the cramped confinement in what were frequently referred to as "pig boats."

In the Pacific, an area of major concern to the U.S. Navy, the lack of air conditioning made life miserable. Heat and humidity climbed to oppressive levels, while limited refrigeration reduced meals to canned goods after the first few days. Freshwater was scarce; washing was a rare luxury to contend with salt-caked sweat and prickly heat. There were two toilets, but their high-pressure air system for flushing was so complex, it discouraged the crew, and constipation became a serious occupational hazard. Officers and men alike preferred to wait for the submarine to surface, then answer the call of nature over the rail. Submariners the world over had to endure so much hardship that an aspirant for submarine service underwent extensive physical and psychological examination.

S-16

S-16 (SS-121) was built to U.S. Navy design by the Lake Torpedo Boat Company at Bridgeport, Connecticut, and was commissioned in December 1920. When she was launched, the 231-foot submarine was the largest vessel of her type in the U.S. Navy, with a beam of 21 feet 10 inches and surface displacement of 876 tons, 1,092 tons submerged. Her surface speed was 15 knots, submerged 11 knots, and her operating depth was 200 feet. The submarine had a complement of 4 officers and 34 enlisted men.

The new S-boat was armed with four bow torpedo tubes and one four-inch deck gun that could be used only against an unarmed or lightly armed vessel. The forward deck was enlarged for servicing the gun, leaving S-16, like other S boats, with submerged speed reduced because of the added bulk.

The new submarine spent the next four years in the Far East (Philippines, Hong Kong, and China). From 1925 to 1928 she operated along the California coast, the following seven years in the Panama Canal area. S-16 was decommissioned at Philadelphia in May 1935. The threat of war brought the 20-year-old veteran back into service in December 1940. During World War II she made defensive patrols off St. Thomas and the Panama Canal Zone. She also patrolled off Martinique and Guadelupe to keep Vichy French warships under surveillance. She saw no war action, but 23 other aged and obsolete S-boats saw active duty in the Pacific during World War II.

S-16 was decommissioned for the final time in October 1944, and was stricken from the Navy list the following month. The submarine's military equipment was removed before she was sunk as a target on April 3, 1945, southwest of Key West, Florida.

Diving *S-16*

S-16 lies in about 250 feet of water, but the deck is at approximately 235 feet. The submarine has a 15° list to starboard. Because of her depth, very little has been recovered by divers. The conning tower hatch cover is gone, but divers cannot enter without removing their double tanks—not a wise move at that depth. However, a diver can peer inside for a view of the submarine's controls and gauges. The extreme depth makes this a hazardous dive and bottom time is limited.

Billy Deans of Key West Divers, Inc. is the only dive-boat operator we know who will take divers to *S-16*. He will do so only if they are experienced wreck divers and he knows them well enough to assess their underwater skills.

S-16 was intentionally sunk in about 250 feet of water. (Photo courtesy of the National Archives.)

A diver alongside S-16's *hull, the largest vessel of her type in the U.S. Navy when launched.* (Photo by Tom Ford.)

Conning tower of S-16 *at a depth of about 250 feet* (Photo by Tom Ford.)

S-21

S-21 (SS-*126*), designed by the Electric Boat Company at New London, Connecticut, was slightly smaller than *S-16*. Her length was 219 feet 3 inches with a beam of 20 feet 8 inches. That made her 11 feet 9 inches shorter, with 1-foot 2 inches less beam. She displaced 854 tons on the surface and 1,062 tons submerged. The submarine was built by the Bethlehem Shipbuilding Corporation at Quincy, Massachusetts. Her armament and complement was the same as *S-16*.

S-21 was commissioned in August 1921, but was decommissioned for return to the builder seven months later. She was recommissioned the following year, and operated off the northeastern U.S. coast and the Panama Canal Zone until 1930. For the following eight years the submarine operated from Pearl Harbor. From 1938 to December 1941 she was at New London.

Two days after the Japanese attacked Pearl Harbor, *S-21* got underway for the Panama Canal Zone. She conducted defensive patrols, and participated in the search and rescue operations for *S-26*, which had been accidentally rammed by another Navy warship.

In September 1942, when she was decommissioned and transferred to Britain, the Royal Navy gave her the designation *P.553*. As newer and more advanced submarines became available the old S-boats were retired.

S-21 *was launched on August 18, 1920 at the Bethlehem Shipbuilding Corp., Quincy, Massachusetts.* (Photo courtesy of the Submarine Force Library and Museum.)

Britain returned *S-21* to the U.S. Navy and she was sunk as a target for aircraft submarine detection training on March 23, 1945. The wreck is about three miles southeast of Halfway Rock in Casco Bay, Maine, at 43° 36′53 N, 69° 59′24 W.

Salvage

The submarine, in about 160 feet of water, was salvaged in 1963 by four Massachusetts scuba divers, Burt Mason, Robert W. Sullivan, Robert Wallace, and Albert Prejean.

The four joined forces in a professional salvage operation. Mason, an experienced marine salvor had been a heating engineer in Connecticut until he responded to an advertisement and learned to dive. In his words, he "... became active in the scrap business." He had earlier located *S-21* while he was searching for a side-paddle-wheeler, that was reportedly sunk in Casco Bay around the turn of the century. He had also salvaged on the German submarine *U-853* in 1960, and the U.S. submarine *G-1* in 1962.

S-21, is on a hard bottom, almost keel up, with her conning tower on the under side of the wreck. The salvors could not easily penetrate the interior of the submarine, forcing Mason to blast an opening in her hull with dynamite. He established the mission objective to be the recovery of marketable metals such as bronze and copper. Sullivan has estimated that they brought up about a fifth of the submarine as chunks of scrap. Lead from the submarine's batteries was also salvaged.

The salvage operation ceased when the 26-year-old Albert Prejean, from Dedham, Massachusetts drowned while working on the submarine. Even though *S-21* was salvaged, most of the hull is relatively intact. There is no record of sport diving on the wreck and no dive boat charter operators take divers to the wreck site.

S-21 entering the Portsmouth (N.H.) Navy Yard. The submarine served in both the U.S. and British navies during World War II. After 25 years of service, she was sunk as a test target at Casco Bay, Maine in 1945. (Photo courtesy of Mrs. Paul Sherman.)

CHAPTER 6

S-37—
Antique Hero

Location: off San Diego, California
Approximate depth of water: 20 to 40 feet
Visibility: poor
Current: little, but frequently a strong surge
Access: boat

No matter how rigid the discipline, rules invite exceptions. The series "Dive into History" was intended to include only wrecks along the Eastern Seaboard of the United States. That constraint was adopted because those were the wrecks we knew most about. Besides, it was felt that the readers would be mostly eastern sport divers.

The remains of *S-37* lie close to the shore of San Diego, California, far from the Eastern Seaboard, but she is included in this volume for various reasons. Her story is intriguing, reference material was available, the submarine is easily accessible, and "Dive into History" has developed not only nation-wide readership, but international. We have chosen to extend our literary license—this time to the West Coast.

Underwater warfare in the Pacific during the early days of World War II relied upon only 55 submarines, almost equally divided between Hawaii and the Philippines to combat the Japanese. Twelve were old S-boats, post-World War I products of the Navy's early attempts to produce fleet submarines. They were poor candidates for America's first line of defense against overwhelming Nippon naval strength. They were obsolete, worn out, ill equipped for tropical heat and humidity, and armed with unreliable torpedoes.

S-37 was one of those outdated submarines that held the line in the Pacific for the first year of the war, and she did so with distinction. That was a real achievement, considering that she seemed to be held together with Bandaids, constantly in need of repair, and the conditions the crew had to operate under were abominable. One of her officers later wrote, ". . . I am playing cribbage with the skipper, mainly because I don't like to wallow in a sweat-soaked bunk most of the day. I have my elbows on the table near the edge and I hold my cards with my arms at a slight angle so the sweat will drain down my bare arms, without soaking the pile of cards in the center. Overhead is a fine net of gauze to catch the wayward cockroaches which prowl across the top of the wardroom and occasionally fall straight downward. They live in the cork insulation which lines the insides of the submarine's hull. We've killed over 16 million cockroaches in one compartment alone."

The old S-boat refused the role of sacrificial pawn. Instead, she gained national fame as the first U.S. submarine to sink a Japanese destroyer. Before she retired from the battle zone in November 1942, *S-37* also sank an enemy merchant ship, damaged another destroyer, and provided help to the survivors of a Dutch ship that had been sunk.

Construction of *S-37* (SS-*142*) was contracted to the Electric Boat Company on July 17, 1917, 24 years before U.S. entry into World War II. Her keel was laid five months later under subcontract to the Union Iron Works plant of the Bethlehem Steel Shipbuilding Company, San Francisco. Although her contracted completion date was February 17, 1919, the new submarine was not launched until four months later. Her delivery and commissioning were delayed another four years, until July 16, 1923. Whatever caused the delay, the product proved to be worth the wait.

The new submarine, like all S-boats, was intended for long-range operation. She was 219 feet 3 inches long and 20 feet 8 inches abeam, and designed for a maximum speed of 14.5 knots surfaced, 11 knots submerged. Her displacement was 854 tons surfaced, 1,062 tons submerged. She carried a complement of four officers and 34 enlisted men, and was armed with four 21-inch torpedo tubes and one 4-inch deck gun.

Lieutenant Paul R. Glutting was in command of the new S-boat at her commissioning. *S-37* was fitted out at Mare Island, then left San Francisco at the end of July for assignment on August 1, to Submarine division (SubDiv) 17 at San Pedro, California. For the next ten weeks, she engaged in exercises and tests off the southern coast of California. On October 10, in San Pedro

S-37's *main deck swells out at the 4-inch deck gun platform, just forward of the conning tower, a design feature unique to the S-class.* (Photo courtesy of the Naval Historical Center.)

S-37 *emerging from underwater.* (Photo courtesy of the Submarine Force Library and Museum.)

Harbor, an explosion occurred in the aft battery compartment while her batteries were being recharged. The resulting fire, dense smoke, and noxious fumes trapped five men in the inferno. Three were brought out, but only two survived. The two who were left behind perished in the disaster.

The solemn crew made temporary repairs, and returned the boat to Mare Island for completion of the work. On December 19, *S-37* returned to SubDiv 17 at San Pedro. She engaged in Canal Zone and Caribbean Fleet exercises until early April, 1924. SubDiv 17 then returned, first to San Pedro then San Francisco, for transfer to the Asiatic Fleet. For the next 16 years, *S-37* operated out of Cavite, on Luzon, ranging through the Philippines, Netherlands East Indies and the coast of China. When the Japanese struck Pearl Harbor, she was in Manila Bay—but not for long.

World War II

S-37 conducted patrols of Philippine bays and straits for three weeks after war was declared, searching for evidence to confirm rumored Japanese landings. Then she headed south to Panay and the Japanese-held Jolo Island, off the coast of Borneo. Her progress was plagued by fire and leaking air supply piping, evidence of her aging. She headed for Port Darwin one month after the war started, but was ordered to the Dutch naval base at Soerabaja, Java. She arrived there on January 23, 1942, after two weeks of searching diligently for Japanese transports and merchant ships to attack, while steering clear of enemy destroyers.

S-37 headed for Makassar Strait, between Borneo and Celebes, on February 2, with Lieutenant James Dempsey in command. Since January 11, Japanese forces had moved onto the two islands. Every occupation requires support services, so it was expected that enemy transports and cargo vessels would abound in the area. By February 6, the S-boat was patrolling the southern approaches to Makassar City, on Celebes, a probable target for the Japanese. Two days later, at 6 p.m. on February 8, the S-boat sighted a speeding destroyer headed her way. Dempsey correctly assumed that it was the advance guard for other Japanese vessels. The destroyer passed without incident; transports and supply ships were more desirable targets.

Less than 15 minutes later, three more destroyers came into view at a distance of 8,000 yards, but no transports. The submarine was preparing to move against them, when four more destroyers were sighted only 4,000 yards away. Behind them were the outlines of three large ships that must have been transports. Jubilation aboard the S-boat was short lived, because the in-line formation of the destroyers provided excellent screening for the transports. *S-37,* however, was eager for action. She went after the destroyers, firing one torpedo at each.

The third torpedo struck its target midships. Smoke erupted from between the stacks of the enemy warship, her decks buckled about 20 feet higher than her bow and stern and *S-37*'s first victim, the Japanese Imperial

Navy's destroyer *Natushio,* exploded and sank. It was the first Japanese destroyer to be sunk by an American submarine, an antiquated S-boat.

The fourth destroyer sighted the submarine as the fourth torpedo was fired. The destroyer turned starboard, an effective evasive maneuver that put her on course to take retribution on *S-37.* The submarine quickly submerged, and prepared for the depth charges that were sure to come. For one and a half hours the three remaining enemy destroyers dropped their charges at 10 to 15 minute intervals, with no serious damage to *S-37.* She ran silent while the destroyers were overhead, and sought sanctuary 267 feet deep during the ordeal, perhaps deeper than enemy assessment of her capability. The Japanese warships finally gave up the search and moved on. When *S-37* surfaced, there were no signs of the enemy.

Two hours after her success, *S-37* reloaded and resumed her search for targets. She remained in Makassar Strait for the next eight days. Lieutenant Dempsey was convinced that it would be even more fruitful for his mission. Several more enemy ships were sighted, but the old S-boat could not match their speed. Another destroyer was attacked and fired upon, with nothing to report but a miss because the defective torpedoes sank before reaching the target.

S-37 headed south, to patrol the Lombok and Badoeng Straits until Dempsey received orders to return to Soerabaja. He proceeded west along the Bali coast with a tell-tale oil slick trailing 2,000 yards behind, leaving the S-boat an easy prey for any watchful enemy lookout. She was undetected by three enemy destroyers only three miles off, then surfaced to make temporary repairs that reduced the tell-tale oil leak. Later the same morning another destroyer was sighted, but it apparently failed to spot the reduced oil slick. Later, as *S-37* was submerged and traveling cautiously, a destroyer was heard off the starboard beam. Depth charges and aerial bombs followed, and she dove to 150 feet, although the greater depth would aggravate the persistent oil leak.

Two hours and 45 minutes after it started, the depth charge attack was interrupted by anti-aircraft fire. After 45 minutes, three more depth charges were dropped. The Japanese search continued for another 3 hours and 15 minutes. Then the pinging ceased. Fifteen minutes later, *S-37* cautiously came up to periscope depth. The destroyer was 3,000 yards off; choppy seas had obliterated the oil slick.

The next day *S-37* reached the Soerabaja Navy Yard. Repairs started immediately, but before they could be completed she was ordered out because the Japanese were moving on Java. Parts, stores, and supplies were taken on and the repairs in process were completed by the submarine's crew. She got underway on her port engine only, and cleared port with the starboard engine still being worked on. The old submarine limped north to patrol between Bawean Island and the western channel into Soerabaja

Roads. Meanwhile the Battle of the Java Sea had just provided the Japanese with an important naval victory. Two Japanese cruisers and three destroyers were sighted on February 28, as they withdrew from that encounter. All thoughts of attack by the submarine were dispelled as she struggled to maintain depth control.

At about noon the same day, a 50-foot open boat was sighted. It carried Allied survivors from the Dutch cruiser *De Ruyter*. The submarine could not accommodate all, but she did take on American sailors who were on board. Provisions were transferred to the survivors, and the boat's location was transmitted in code to initiate rescue efforts.

S-37 was sighted later the same afternoon as she attempted to attack an enemy formation. She submerged, and endured a combined depth charging and aerial bombing that certainly weakened her aging hull, but did no serious damage.

For another week the submarine remained in the area, under frequent depth charge and aerial bomb attacks that further weakened her mechanical and electrical components. An oil leak through the engine room hatch was held under control, but it still leaked three gallons an hour, more than enough to betray her underwater position. On March 6, she headed for western Australia, leaving an oil slick that would have led an observer south toward Lombok Strait before it branched east, then south again. The submarine managed to clear the East Indies by March 11, and arrived at Fremantle on the 19th.

In April, she proceeded to Brisbane, where she was assigned to Task Force 42. A thorough overhaul prepared her for her fifth war patrol, to New Guinea, on June 22. By the end of the month she was patrolling St. George Channel in the Bismark archipelago. On July 7, she shifted to the island of New Britain, to patrol the coast off Lambert Point. The next day she sighted a Japanese cargo ship, under escort by a submarine chaser. Three torpedoes were unleashed on the merchant ship. All hit the target, sending the 2,776-ton *Tenzan Maru* plummeting to the bottom. The submarine submerged and escaped retaliation by the enemy sub chaser with evasive action that took her on a northerly course, away from the scene of her second sinking.

S-37 resumed patrol of the Bismark Islands. On July 14, what seemed to be a minor fire in the starboard main motor was quickly extinguished. But from then on, electrical and mechanical failures were frequent. The next week was filled with uncertainty that *S-37* might not make it back to Australia. The strain continued until July 21, when she finally reached the security of Brisbane harbor.

Almost one month later, on August 17, the ancient S-boat left on her sixth war mission, supporting the Guadalcanal campaign with a defensive patrol in the Savo Island area. On September 2, a column of four enemy destroyers was sighted north of Savo, and *S-37* added to her laurels with a damaging torpedo hit on one of the four. On September 13, she returned to Brisbane.

On October 19, *S-37* left Brisbane for Noumea, New Caledonia, to serve in defense of that important naval base. Another fire, this time in her port main motor, more mechanical failures, and ballast tank trouble were more than local maintenance skills could handle. Besides, fuel was scarce, and it made more sense to pump what there was into the more modern submarines. The S-boat left for Pearl Harbor, then San Diego, where she underwent an extensive overhaul during the winter of 1943. She ended her career there, serving as an antisubmarine warfare training ship through 1944.

On February 6, 1945, *S-37* was decommissioned and stripped in preparation for towing to a target site for aerial bombs. En route, the tow line broke, and the submarine went aground off Coronado. The Navy sold salvage rights to a private company that used flotation tanks to refloat her, but again the tow line broke. The old S-boat submerged for the last time, in 20 to 40 feet of water only 200 yards from the shore of Imperial Beach, just above the Mexican border.

Diving *S-37*

S-37 is so shallow and so close to shore that the advantages of unlimited diving time are offset by surge and poor visibility. The only time to attempt the dive is under extremely calm conditions. They would most likely occur in the months of January or February, when a west swell calms the waters off the southern California coast.

The submarine is on her port side, canted at an angle of about 45°. Her conning tower is usually about 10 feet below the surface, but an unusually low tide exposes it above water. The deck is at about 15 feet above the bottom. The submarine is intact, and divers have declared that the sturdy S-boat should last for another century. Diving is usually from private boats, even though the site is only 200 yards off the beach, because it is difficult to locate the wreck from shore.

The open conning tower invites entry. It is the highest point of the wreck, but so high that it is always in the midst of surge. As early as 1976, divers were warned not to loiter near the hatch because "strong seasurges can suck a man inside before he knows it." More recently, divers have learned that the surge is indeed strong, but they have braved the turbulence to enter the hatch, with happy results. The interior of the conning tower looks forebodingly dark from above, but once inside, the gloom is partially dispelled by light streaming through the open hatch.

Many artifacts have been removed in the years since *S-37* settled into the sand. Although the Navy stripped her before her planned use as an aerial bomb target, components that are valuable relics today were left undisturbed.

Scuba divers have removed telegraphs, assorted wheels and gauges, the ship's wheel, and portholes. *S-37* was one of the Navy's pre-World War II submarines that were constructed with six or seven conning tower portholes.

In 1980, several divers salvaged *S-37*. They used a cutting torch to make openings into several compartments to remove artifacts and to allow safe penetration by divers. On one occasion, leaking diesel fuel produced an oil slick that extended down to the Mexican border. The divers entered the torpedo room and found it to be intact. Although there was little sediment to contend with, three feet of jelled diesel fuel had settled to the bottom of the compartment. When a diver entered the compartment, the disturbed diesel fuel reduced visibility to zero. When they surfaced and climbed aboard the dive boat, the oil-covered divers were hosed down with water from a fire hose to remove the diesel fuel from their suits and gear. Even under such adverse conditions the divers removed many artifacts from the compartment, including the four brass torpedo tube doors, each weighing about 450 pounds.

The divers cut an opening into the crew's quarters, and another into the engine room.

One diver noticed light entering the conning tower while he was inside the submarine. The light was entering through six portholes that had not been noticed from outside because steel plates had been welded over S-boat portholes for greater protection. Cutting equipment was again used to remove all six portholes. One diver said that he has spent over 1,000 hours on *S-37* during the last decade.

One of the 65-pound portholes is currently displayed at the Pacific Submarine Museum, one of the museum's few S-boat artifacts. It features a sliding brass cover for protection against depth charges. The curator of the museum, Ray de Yarmin, accepted the gift from Herb Miller, an industrial engineer, naval reservist, and diving enthusiast. Miller, who had recovered the porthole from the submarine, is a member of the California Wreck Divers. His avid interest in old submarines is reflected in the extensive collection of artifacts he has preserved, including *S-37*'s ship's wheel.

The safest access to the submarine's interior is through a three-by-six foot hole that was cut in the crew's quarters for removal of the ship's wheel. Other entry points have been overgrown by marine life. The wreck is dark and filled with sand. Only very experienced divers should attempt access to the interior. One compensation for the problems of diving the wreck is the bounty of lobsters that frequent this old relic of another era. They are there for the taking.

Also for the taking by those who have come to "dive into history" is the historic significance of visiting the stubborn old S-boat that protected the United States with such distinction in the critical, early days of World War II.

CHAPTER 7

S-49—
For the Advanced Diver

Location: Patuxent River, Solomons, Maryland
Approximate depth of water: 125 feet
Visibility: poor to very poor
Current: strong, dive at slack tide
Access: boat

The S-class proved to be a very successful design for the U.S. Navy; 51 boats were constructed at several yards. The last four, built to a new Navy design, were assigned to the Lake Torpedo Boat Company under a construction contract. They were 240 feet long, 21 feet 10 inches abeam, and displaced 990 tons on the surface and 1,230 tons submerged. Power had been increased on later versions of the S-boat, including *S-49,* and a stern torpedo tube was added to the four in the bow. A four-inch deck gun was also part of the armament.

S-49 (SS-*160*) was commissioned in June 1922, the 160th submarine ordered by the Navy. For the next four years she remained in the New London area and participated in experiments, including aerial visibility tests and torpedo development. In 1926, 12 of her crew were gassed in a battery explosion. Four died. The Navy inquiry found that overcharged batteries leaked hydrogen gas. A crewman had accidentally dropped a deck plate and the resulting spark caused the explosion.

In 1927, *S-49* participated in exercises off Florida. She was decommissioned on August 2 of the same year after only five years of service. The submarine was struck from the Navy list on March 21, 1931 in accordance with the London Naval Treaty, which limited the size of ascribing nations' navies. For the next five years she was used as an exhibit at the Great Lakes Exposition in Cleveland. Thousands of people paid 25 cents each to tour the submarine. In 1936, *S-49* was sold to the Boston Iron and Metal Company, Baltimore, Maryland, for $7,666. The submarine was reduced to a hulk, but was not scrapped. Seven years later, the U.S. Navy reacquired the hulk for experimental work at the Naval Mine Warfare Proving Ground (now the Naval Air Test Center), Solomons, Maryland.

S-49 was listed as a piece of equipment, and was not recommissioned. Inventory is kept on a piece of equipment, but not logs or performance records. For that reason, the balance of the submarine's history is uncertain. It is recalled that the hulk was rigged to dive and surface by remote control in mine and sonar tests. It has also been reported that she may have been used in training exercises with the McCann Rescue Chamber to rescue crewmen from a sunken submarine.

It is known that the submarine was sunk in about 125 feet of water in the Patuxent River and at some point was used for training U.S. Navy hardhat divers. Jon Hulburt, an experienced wreck diver and underwater photog-

S-49, one of the last S-boats. These boats formed the backbone of the Navy's submarine force during the 1920s and the early 1930s. (Photo courtesy of the Submarine Force Library and Museum.)

The main switchboard inside S-49*'s control room.* (Photo courtesy of the Submarine Force Library and Museum.)

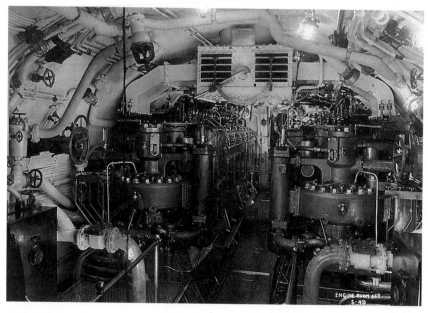

S-49*'s engine room.* (Photo courtesy of the Submarine Force Library and Museum.)

Above: S-49's forward torpedo room. Below: the stern torpedo room. (Photos courtesy of the Submarine Force Library and Museum.)

rapher, recovered a brass, hardhat diving boot on the wreck. At some time, either before or after she was sunk, the port side conning tower was cut away, the four bow torpedo tubes were plated over and the single stern tube was blocked by Navy divers who welded a metal bar over the opening. Hatch covers were removed and the openings covered with circular steel plates that were welded onto the hull.

At some time in her past, other modifications were made on *S-49*. The conning tower of S-class submarines was simply a watertight trunk to an elevated bridge, where the boat could be "conned" while on the surface. It was not a control room, as it was on later boats. The submarine was commanded from the control room below the conning tower. However, sport divers have found that a large hole was cut in the port side of *S-49*'s conning tower. Also, *S-49*'s conning tower contained instruments and controls that were normally located in the control room of other S-boats. The periscopes and screw-propellers had been removed prior to sinking. The hulk was still in use as late as the 1970s. Considering the very bad visibility and the strong current, *S-49* must have been ideal for training Navy divers to perform in adverse conditions. However, they are far from ideal for sport divers.

Diving *S-49*

In 1985, Mike Moore, an experienced wreck diver from Baltimore, was talking to a waterman who had spent most of his life on the Bay. "You looking for shipwrecks," he said, "you ought to go looking for the Nazi submarine." That caught Moore's interest. Another waterman later confirmed the story "there's a Nazi submarine on the bottom of the Patuxent River. It's got $50,000 in gold and Hitler's body on board!"

Moore told us, "I've never put much faith in 'Nazi Sub' rumors, but I do check them out. Most of them stem from one of two sources. After the First World War, *U-117*, a war prize, stranded while under tow and remained aground for over a year. After World War II, several U-boats were brought into the bay for testing . . . all of them have been accounted for. One reason I've tracked the various U-boat rumors is that they might lead me to other wrecks. For over 30 years I had hoped to find an S-class submarine. The S-class boats, could easily be mistaken for a U-boat. None of the S-boats were saved by the Navy. My fervent hope was that the 'Nazi sub' in the Patuxent River might be an S-boat."

He visited the Naval Historical Center in Washington and went through the files of individual S-boats. Fortunately, he started with the last, *S-51*, and worked backwards. He hit paydirt with *S-49*. The official record stated she had been sold for scrap in 1930 to comply with the London Naval Treaty. A footnote, however, stated the Navy had re-purchased her as a "miscellaneous test object" to be used at the Naval Mine Warfare Proving Ground. That proving ground, since abandoned, had been less than a mile from where the watermen said the U-boat was located!

He then checked the navigation chart of the Patuxent River and found a wreck symbol in 130 feet of water. Again the site was close to the one given to him by the watermen. The location was sheltered from rough weather, so he decided to search for the wreck the next time he was in the area with nowhere else to dive.

That opportunity came on July 4, 1986. He had been diving wrecks about 20 miles south of the submarine's reported location when strong south winds, the worst on the bay, forced him to suspend diving. He trailored his boat over to the Patuxent River and started searching for the submarine. Within an hour he had a target on the depth sounder, in about 125 feet of water with 112 feet over the wreck.

Moore spent six hours trying to grapple onto the wreck before calling it a day. He was almost certain that he had found a submarine. Submarines, in general, are hard to hook. Their smooth sides, designed to slide past nets and mine cables, provide little for a grapple to catch. He later told us, "this wreck was particularly difficult since she lay with her axis parallel to the prevailing current. Time and time again the anchor just slid down her length and off the end." Finally, on Thanksgiving weekend 1986, he tried a different tack. He replaced the grappling hook with a more conventional anchor, and timed his attempt for slack water. He dropped the anchor on top of the wreck and felt it slide off into the sand. He let out a lot of scope in the anchor line and sent another diver, Peter Kessler, down to run a search pattern. As Kessler, descending the anchor line in bad visibility, neared the bottom his shoulder brushed the wreck. It was a submarine. He tied a buoyed mooring line into the top of the conning tower. Moore left the mooring in for three days while he shuttled divers to and from the wreck.

Over the three days he recognized features that identified the find. The submarine's main deck swelled out at the gun platform, a design feature unique to the S-class. She had five torpedo tubes with the stern tube placed high. Only S-48 through S-51 had that feature. Her exhaust ports were compatible with those S-boats. S-48, S-50, and S-51 were all accounted for. He had an S-boat and she was S-49.

Moore still hears rumors of Nazi subs in the bay and he keeps checking them out. Who knows what he might find next?

S-49 sits on her keel in the middle of the river, with a slight list to starboard, her bow pointing downstream. The LORAN numbers are 27493.0 and 42232.0. Magnetic bearings are 144° on the Point Patience light, 099° on the radio tower farthest out on Point Patience, and 329° on the headland just upstream. The state maintains an excellent launching ramp on the north side of the Patuxent River where Route 4 crosses. The submarine is about 0.9 nautical mile from the ramp, just upstream from Point Patience.

Caution

Diving *S-49* is for the advanced wreck diver only. Strong currents and heavy boat traffic in the area make a trail line a necessity. Due to bad visibility and blackwater, divers must use a powerful light, with a backup in case the primary light fails. Using a light provides visibility of about five feet on a good day. It is a night dive regardless of the hour. Gary Gentile, an experienced wreck diver, author, and underwater photographer, wrote in *Scubapro Diving and Snorkeling* that on one *S-49* dive he intentionally dropped down the anchor line with his light turned off. He wanted to savor the full effects of darkness. He wrote, "At 50 feet I had my last look at my gauges. After that, even the luminescent dials refused to glow. Gripping the taut rope tightly, so as not to be swept into limbo by the downstream current, I pulled forward, reaching out with one hand then the other. My hold on the anchor line was my only touch with reality . . . My face mask banged into something solid. I clutched the anchor line as if my life depended on it. With my free hand I grappled for the light held onto my wrist by a lanyard. I worked my fingers along until I felt the switch. And then there was light—but not a lot of it."

S-49 is a serious dive for the advanced diver.

CHAPTER 8

Bass—
Torpex Target

Location: 8.2 miles south of Block Island, Rhode Island
Approximate depth of water: 155 feet
Visibility: good
Current: little to moderate
Access: boat

The United States submarine *Bass* (SS-*164*) owed her existence to the effective blockade maintained by the British over German merchant shipping during World War I. Desperate for war materials, the Germans devised a plan to run that blockade with large freight-carrying U-boats. On July 9, 1916, the first of those underwater merchant vessels electrified the world with the first trans-Atlantic crossing by a German submarine. Arrival of Germany's freight-carrying submarine *Deutschland* at Baltimore, Maryland stirred consternation in American defense circles. The demonstrated capability of U-boats to cross the Atlantic exposed the entire Eastern Seaboard to the potential for German military action.

Deutschland measured 213 feet, about the same length as a military U-boat of the time, but with a much broader beam to accommodate cargo, and designed to remain at sea for three to five months. The cargo unloaded

The German U-boat Deutschland *was the first submarine cargo carrier to cross the Atlantic Ocean.* (Photo courtesy of the Submarine Force Library and Museum.)

at Baltimore included chemicals, dyestuffs, precious stones, and mail. For the return to Germany, *Deutschland's* compartments were crammed with one million dollars worth of crude rubber, zinc, silver, copper, and nickle. Critical as those materials were to Germany's armaments industry, the propaganda success of breaking Britain's blockade with long-range merchant U-boats was even more important.

The publicity did not escape attention by the U.S. Navy, concerned over the vast distances to be covered in fulfilling its commitments, particularly in the Pacific. *Deutschland's* success underlined the urgent need for larger, longer-range U.S. submarines. The merchant U-boats ultimately proved to be financially unsound, and the Germans converted them to combat U-boats—the same concept the U.S. Navy had in mind.

Military appropriations encounter the least opposition during wartime. Immediately after United States entry into World War I, a program was funded to develop an American version of Germany's merchant U-boats—but larger and with greater operating range. The development produced large submarines for the U.S. Navy—the V-class.

The second of the new vessels was launched at the Portsmouth Navy Yard in an impressive ceremony on December 27, 1924—not as *Bass* but, in accordance with existing practice, as *V-2.* The new submarine was 341

Civilians tour the new submarines Bass *and* Bonita. *Their shark-nosed bows had a stem anchor and their conning towers were equipped with portholes.* (Photo courtesy of the National Archives.)

feet 6 inches long, 60% longer than Germany's merchant U-boats; her 2,620 tons submerged displacement was 73% greater; her beam was 27 feet, 7 inches; and her draft was 15 feet 11 inches. Those impressive dimensions accommodated more powerful engines, more durable machinery, improved habitability, and larger fuel bunkers than the earlier U.S. Navy S-class. All contributed to the new submarine's 12,000 miles operating range. Armament included one 3-inch deck gun, two machine guns, and six torpedo tubes—four forward and two aft—with twelve torpedoes.

V-2 was commissioned September 26, 1925, with a complement of 80 officers and seamen, under command of Lt. Commander G.A. Road. Her first assignment was with Submarine Division 20, cruising the Atlantic coast and the Caribbean. The division transferred to San Diego in November 1927, and for the next 10 years the vessel operated on the Pacific coast, Hawaii, and again in the Caribbean. When the Navy changed submarine identification from numeral designations to types of fish on March 9, 1931, *V-2* was renamed *Bass.*

Six years later, *Bass* went into reserve at Philadelphia after 13 years of peacetime service. In response to the threat of war with Germany, she was recommissioned on September 5, 1940, for assignment to Submarine

U.S. submarine Bass *before her unsuccessful conversion to a cargo carrier. The boat was awkward and difficult to control while submerged.* (Photo courtesy of the Naval Historical Center.)

Division 6, Atlantic Fleet. In November she sailed for Coco Solo, Canal Zone, and served there until hostilities broke out with Japan. She was reassigned to Division 31, Squadron 3, and made four war patrols in 1942, with no enemy encounters. However, a disastrous fire in her aft battery room crippled *Bass* as effectively as though she had been a combat victim. The spreading flames quickly engulfed the aft torpedo room and the starboard main motor room, consuming air, and releasing toxic fumes. Asphyxiation claimed the lives of 25 enlisted men out of a crew of 80—a major disaster.

The crippled submarine, with what remained of her crew, was escorted into the Gulf of Dulce, Costa Rica by U.S.S. *Antaeus* for temporary repairs. Then, *Bass* headed for Philadelphia for more permanent refitting before assignment to New London, Connecticut, for secret experiments off Block Island, Rhode Island. A year later, she underwent three months of repair at Philadelphia, then returned to New London, this time to operate between Long Island, New York, and Block Island—not much of a challenge for a submarine with an operating range of 12,000 miles.

Bass was used at the New London Submarine School during the latter part of the war because fleet submarines simply couldn't be spared for school work. There was some thinking that she could be used as a troop transport. *Nautilus* and *Argonaut* had already served in that role against the Japanese on Makin Island. Apparently she wasn't required for that purpose.

President Franklin Roosevelt insisted that *Bass's* torpedo rooms and aft engine room be converted into cargo space to transform her into a cargo carrier like Germany's U-boat *Deutschland*. With the renovations, it became quite a trip to proceed aft through the boat—one went through a watertight door to face a solid wall, the side of the cargo tank. It was a challenging obstacle course to climb a ladder to the top of the tank, crawl between the top of the tank and the hull, and eventually work through the boat.

Removal of the main engines left propulsion to the electric motors, with generator engines for charging the batteries. The generator engines could be switched directly to the electric propulsion motor, but at best, top surface speed was five to seven knots—not much. Like *Deutschland*, *Bass* failed as a cargo carrier. There was no practical use for the obsolete submarine. She was worn out, used up, barely able to run, and could hardly dive. Chief Motor Machinists Mate I.R. "Bud" Byron 23 years later stated, "What was particularly alarming was to dive the *Bass*. Coming from the Pacific war and many years on fleet subs, most of the crew like myself were used to crash diving, leveling off at periscope depth . . . in a matter of seconds. On the *Bass* it was something else again. Being so big, the slightest down angle would be too much for the diving planes to control and the screws would come out of the water. Another problem was leakage. No sooner than she would get below the surface, one could bet that someone in the auxiliary engine room would yell for help to try to close an engine exhaust valve or some other cranky fitting that was letting the ocean pour in. Usually the leaks had to be repaired and it meant surfacing, which used most of the compressed air and required hours of running the air compressors to charge the air banks again . . . the *Bass* simply was no great fighting submarine. I hate to think what a severe depth charging could have done to her."

The Navy needed a target for testing new, experimental equipment and *Bass* was selected. She was decommissioned, stripped, and designated a hulk on March 3, 1945. Her armament had been fired only in practice. It was probably a blessing that she had been spared from combat. The new class of submarine was a bitter disappointment. The large submarines were notably difficult to maneuver submerged, and the diesel-electric motors proved undependable. They never delivered the 21 knots surface speed for which they had been designed. But *Bass* would not require speed for her new assignment.

Test Subject for a New Explosive

Depth charges were critical weapons in Britain's war against the U-boat throughout World War II. Their effect on Germany's underwater fleet was multiplied by the surprise of delivery by aircraft. As early as May 1942, Britain's Wellington bombers added torpex depth charges that were 50% more destructive than conventional explosives. By the end of the war, 47%

of all U-boat sinkings would be attributed to Allied aircraft, a far cry from the relatively ineffectual role of the airplane in World War I anti-submarine action. Early in the war, Admiral Karl Doenitz, commander-in-chief, U-boats scoffed, "An aircraft can no more kill a U-boat than a crow can kill a mole." He learned otherwise.

Torpex is a highly volatile mixture of TNT, aluminum and RDX (cyclonite). Cyclonite, discovered in 1899, was too unstable for military munitions, but the British had reduced the risk by combining it with beeswax. The scarcity of beeswax made it essential to find an alternative solution that would keep production flowing for the air war against Hitler's U-boats.

Britain turned to American military chemists for help, and got it—but not before U.S. Army tests revealed that the powerful explosive should be rejected because it was too volatile. Only Rear Admiral W.H.P. Blandy, Chief of the U.S. Navy Bureau of Ordnance, supported its use by the U.S. military. His confidence was justified when a substitute for beeswax and an improved method of production were developed. The powerful new explosive was then loaded into Mark 24 depth charges for testing to determine whether *Bass* could survive its destructive force.

The death knell sounded for *Bass* on March 18, 1945. Fuel tanks were drained to protect the waters from pollution and she was towed to 41° 01′ N, 71° 32′ W—8.2 nautical miles south of Block Island. Chief Mate Byron recalled, "We stood on the dock and watched her go and there was rejoicing in the ranks of the submariners that day."

Bass was left anchored on the surface in normal diving trim, with hatches closed and dogged down to seal all nine compartments.

A PBY-5A aircraft of the Anti-Submarine Development Detachment at the Quonset Point, Rhode Island, Naval Air Station loaded two Mark 24 torpex-filled mines aboard and headed for Block Island at 12:00 noon. Conditions were ideal—ceiling unlimited, visibility 20 miles, surface winds five to six knots from northwest, and sea calm.

As the PBY passed over Block Island and sighted *Bass,* the plane descended to 200 feet at a speed of 115 knots. It was 12:30 p.m. when the PBY released its first mine, preset for a depth of 120 feet. It struck the surface 150 feet off the submarine's starboard beam, slightly aft of amidships—but no explosion followed.

Thirteen minutes later, the second mine was released from an altitude of 150 feet, set for a depth of 45 feet. It hit about 100 feet off the starboard beam, midway between the conning tower and stern. A long 44 seconds passed. Then a tremendous detonation forward of the conning tower shot plumes of seawater high into the air on both sides of the hull. A second explosion at the stern followed almost immediately, and a large boil of water and air broke the surface to starboard. The Navy attributed the second explosion to countermining of the first mine by detonation of the second.

Sinking of Bass *by aircraft of the Anti-submarine Development Detachment. After an explosion off the stern, a large boil of water and air broke the surface to starboard and the submarine started to settle by the bow.* (Photo courtesy of the Naval Historical Center.)

The submarine started to settle by the bow within 20 seconds; in less than a minute, the forward deck and conning tower were out of sight. *Bass* continued to sink until her bow struck bottom hard, shearing the hull forward of the conning tower in two. The stern slowly settled until, 3 minutes and 40 seconds after the first detonation, the target submarine disappeared.

No debris, only a few air bubbles that would soon be gone and residue from the torpex explosions, marked the grave of U.S.S. *Bass.* The Navy's epitaph for the 20-year-old submarine that had never achieved its potential as a warship was appropriate in its brevity: "The rapid sinking of the hulk of the *Bass* indicates that the lethal characteristics of the Mark 24 mine are adequate."

The two sections of the wreck settled upright on the bottom. As marine organisms accumulated, the hull developed into an artificial reef, the destiny of every sunken vessel. A wide variety of marine life soon converged on the site—and fishermen were quick to follow. One, Paul Forsburg, an operator of several charter fishing boats from Montauk, New York, took charters to the wreck for years of bountiful fishing with no idea of its identity.

The Navy, however, had not forgotten *Bass* nor her location. Plans to buoy her were considered in December 1948, then abandoned. Later, in April 1958, it was proposed that she be raised for use in atomic weapons testing in the Pacific. That idea was also abandoned. Then, Nickolas

Zimkowski, of Newport, Rhode Island, paid the Navy $1,278 for scrap salvage rights in 1962, but he never tried to bring the submarine to the surface.

Diving *Bass*

Four years later, Paul Forsburg had added scuba charters to his fishing charter service. In June 1966, he scheduled ten divers for a trip to the Italian passenger liner *Andrea Doria.* The charter included noted underwater photographer Michael deCamp and George Hoffman, a well-known New Jersey dive boat captain. After everyone was aboard, a one-day delay was called because of a bad storm. Forsburg suggested a dive on the unknown wreck as an alternative because it was much closer to shore. That was disappointing news for the divers who were anticipating the glamorous *Doria,* but the prospect of diving a wreck before anyone else was exciting. All wreck divers hold the dream of one day being the first to dive a newly discovered wreck.

DeCamp and Hoffman swam down the anchor line on an exploratory dive and found poor visibility that discouraged anyone else from diving. But while they were down, the two groped along the wreck, feeling its outlines. The hull was rounded. Could it be a submarine? The group returned on a follow-up charter to find out. In visibility that was much improved, deCamp and Hoffman confirmed that the find was indeed a submarine—broken into two sections. Several days later, one of the divers contacted Joseph A. Palmer of Cumberland, Rhode Island, an insurance underwriter whose hobby was collecting historical data on U.S. submarines. Palmer concluded that the wreck was probably *Bass,* deliberately sunk by the Navy in 1945.

Hoffman and deCamp again chartered Forsburg's boat to explore the hull for clues to its positive identification. Bill Hoodiman, a New Jersey diver, fashioned a wrench with a long handle for leverage to undog the hatch aft of the conning tower. He stood on the deck and walked the wrench around, apparently without result. Hoodiman left and deCamp and Hoffman approached the hatch. Without warning, air, trapped in the submarine for 21 years, literally blew the loosened, spring-loaded hatch open.

When the turbulence of escaping air subsided, deCamp and Hoffman hung onto the hull for dear life to keep from being sucked into the compartment as surrounding water gushed in. The following day, the two divers entered the compartment. They were startled to discover that when they stood upright, the water level was only up to their necks; the upper part of the interior was dry. Some hatches have a five-foot sleeve extending into the interior. Above the sleeve, the compartment still contained air that had remained undisturbed for more than two decades.

The submarine was identified by divers penetrating the wreck in 1966. They recovered a white wooden box with "U.S.S. Bass" stenciled in black on the side. It contained an electrical armature. (Photo by Michael deCamp.)

John Dudas displays a helm he recovered in 1966 from the submarine's conning tower. A spare helm was found in the ship's bow by Bill Palmer 23 years later. (Photo by Michael deCamp.)

The search for identification was rewarding; the divers recovered a white, wooden box, containing a replacement electrical armature, with *Bass* stenciled on the outside. Joseph Palmer was right; they had found the submarine that had been sacrificed to prove that her own kind could be destroyed by a powerful new weapon.

The submarine, sitting upright on the white sand bottom, is not a regular dive site for the average scuba diver because of the depth, approximately 140 feet to the deck, about 155 feet to the sand. Poor light penetration at that depth often makes the dive a dark one. However, occasionally a diver swimming forward of the conning tower can view the broken off bow section—about 50 feet away. The hull break is just forward of a bulkhead, leaving the bow section open for easy penetration as far as the next bulkhead. Divers can also enter the forward engine room where the hatch was removed. There is very little room to maneuver in the engine room because of the mass of machinery. A diver may become disoriented and find it difficult to find the exit. Extreme caution must be exercised to ensure safe exit when penetrating any wreck, especially within the close quarters of a submarine.

Sport diving is exciting and rewarding, but if needless risk endangers life the fun is not worth the penalty.

Bill Palmer (no relation to Joseph Palmer) holds Bass' *spare helm, which he recovered from the bow in 1989.* (Photo by H. Keatts.)

CHAPTER 9

Tarpon—
Fighting Fish

Location: about 22 miles from Okracoke Inlet, North Carolina
Approximate depth of water: 145 feet
Visibility: good to excellent
Current: little to strong on the surface, little on the wreck
Access: boat

Sport fishermen know the tarpon to be a strong, skilled, and agile fighter, noted for the outstanding speed and acrobatic ability that carries it out of the water in leaps that can be 10 feet high and 20 feet long.

The U.S. Navy's *Tarpon* (SS-*175*) earned an equally enviable reputation by her World War II record. Twelve war patrols in the Pacific earned seven battle stars for the P-class submarine. She sank four enemy vessels including the German Raider *Michel,* an armed merchant ship that had preyed upon Allied shipping, first in the Atlantic, then in the Pacific. *Tarpon's* other sinkings included two Japanese transports and a patrol boat. Five merchant ships were damaged. Her sixth patrol accounted for 27,910 tons sunk, the best record of any U.S. submarine to that date.

Tarpon was the second of that name to serve in the U.S. Navy. On November 17, 1911 the pre-World War I submarine *Tarpon* (SS-*14*) was

Tarpon was the first American submarine to sink a German ship in World War II, when she torpedoed the auxiliary cruiser Michel *on March 2, 1943.* (Photo courtesy of the Submarine Force Library and Museum.)

renamed *C-3*. The second *Tarpon* owed her existence to pre-World War II international tension, pro-Navy leanings in Washington, and President Franklin Roosevelt's interest in creating jobs to relieve the unemployment of the Depression years. Congress approved funds in 1933 for a long-range naval build-up that included construction of the aircraft carriers *Yorktown, Enterprise,* and *Wasp,* 7 battleships, 11 cruisers, 108 destroyers, and 26 submarines. All of the submarines were to be commissioned between 1935 and 1939.

P-Class Boats

The first ten submarines, launched between 1935 and 1937 were P-class (*Porpoise*-class) boats. The sixteen that followed were slightly longer, heavier, and armed with two additional torpedo tubes. They were *Salmon*- and *Sargo*-class boats that were built in 1938 and 1939. All were powered by new, lightweight, high-performance diesel engines. But what distinguished them from earlier models was far more dramatic. The diesels did not drive the submarine. They operated generators to power electric motors on the surface and to charge batteries for underwater operation. In addition, they were the first all-welded submarines to serve in the U.S. Navy, setting the standard for the mass-production of submarines in World War II.

Inside Tarpon's *control room, looking forward, before she sank off Cape Hatteras.* (Photo courtesy of the Submarine Force Library and Museum.)

Four P-class keels were laid in 1933—*Porpoise* (SS-*172*) and *Pike* (SS-*173*) at the Navy's Portsmouth Yard; Shark and (SS-*174*) *Tarpon* (SS-*175*) at the Groton, Connecticut, Electric Boat Company. Although their names did not follow the P series, *Shark* and *Tarpon* were classified as P-class because they corresponded in design and armament characteristics. They were 298 feet long, 25-foot abeam, 1,316 tons surface displacement, and 1,968 tons submerged. The submarines were rated to submerge to 250 feet. Surface speed was specified as 18 knots, although *Tarpon* achieved 19.5 knots on trials. Cruising range was 11,000 miles at 10 knots while on the surface. Top speed, while submerged, was 8 knots. Underwater operation could be maintained at 5 knots for 10 hours or at minimum speed for as long as 36 hours. Fuel capacity was more than 85,000 gallons. Diving time was 60 seconds.

Armament of the P-class boats included 4 torpedo tubes forward, 2 in the stern, 18 torpedoes, a 3-inch deck gun, and a .50 caliber machine gun. Fire control improvements, air conditioning, and new rescue features provided more effectiveness, comfort and safety for the crew of five officers and 45 crewmen. Oxygen rebreathers called Monsen Lungs enabled men to leave the submarine through escape hatches at depths of 100 feet or more. Forward and aft torpedo room hatches were fitted with new devices to lock on the McCann Rescue Chamber, a rescue diving bell developed by a submariner, Allen Rockwell McCann. Buoys equipped with telephones were carried, to be released by entrapped submariners for communication between themselves and rescuers on the surface. That impressive array of new safety features was a dramatic advance over the S-class submarines (see Chapter 5, *S-5*).

Tarpon's keel was laid on December 22, 1933. She was launched September 4, 1935 sponsored by Miss E.K. Roosevelt, daughter of Assistant Secretary of the Navy Henry L. Roosevelt, and commissioned March 12, 1936 with Lieutenant Leo L. Pace in command.

The new submarine operated out of San Diego and Pearl Harbor for the next three and a half years, first with Submarine Division (Sub-Div) 13, then with Sub-Div 14. *Shark,* the only submarine in the Navy with the same specifications as *Tarpon,* served with her and five other P-boats to make up Sub-Div 14. In October 1939, they were transferred to the Phillipines to augment six older S boats in forming Submarine Squadron Five, potentially the most lethal arm of an otherwise unimpressive Asiatic Fleet. Two years later, Sub-Divs 15 and 16 were transferred from Pearl Harbor to Manila, increasing the Asiatic Force to 29 submarines in five divisions. *Tarpon* was assigned to Sub-Div 203 in October 1941, less than two months before the Japanese air strike on Pearl Harbor.

War Patrols

Tarpon began her first war patrol with Lieutenant Commander W. Weeden, Jr. in command two days after the Japanese attack. That mission was unproductive but her second, under the command of Lieutenant Commander L. Wallace, left a 9,000-ton enemy tanker apparently sinking from two torpedo hits. However, post-war analysis of Japanese records failed to confirm that sinking. Ten days later, on February 11, 1942, four depth charges severely jolted the submarine, damaging her bow planes, rudder angle indicators, and port annunciator. A dive of 235 feet and a hard turn to port were not enough to avoid the four detonations that erupted in rapid succession. The submarine survived the punishing attack, but ran aground later while trying to navigate the treacherous Boling Strait, west of Flores Island. In attempting to navigate the narrow waterway by moonlight early in the morning of February 24, the navigator was misled by a clump of mangrove trees which he mistook for Point Tauk. *Tarpon* ran aground at 12 knots and remained there. No amount of backing, twisting or blowing ballast tanks would free her. Weight was dumped, ammunition jettisoned, fuel oil and fresh water went into the sea and lubricating oil was shifted aft. Still, the grounded submarine would not budge.

Tarpon *was overhauled at Mare Island Navy Yard early in World War II. The large circle in the top photo shows one of two external torpedo tubes added to increase her forward torpedo tubes from four to six. In the bottom photo the lower circle on the conning tower identifies bridge alterations to lower her silhouette. The circle by the stern shows a degaussing cable, added to protect the submarine from mines.* (Photos courtesy of the National Archives.)

A Dutch missionary, H. von den Rulst, the only white man on the nearby island of Adunara, provided information, both good and bad, to the stranded submariners. High tide, the best time to free the submarine, would occur between 4 p.m. and 6 p.m. That was good, but news that Japanese planes had flown over the island each of the past four days made for some anxious moments. That afternoon, on a flood peak tide, with three engines backing at full power and heaving in on the anchor windlass, the submarine slid back into the sea, further damaged but still seaworthy. She returned to Fremantle, Australia, on March 5 to learn that her only sister boat, *Shark* had been sunk by a Japanese warship off Celebes Island, with the loss of her entire crew (see Chapter 13).

Tarpon's third and fourth patrols were both unproductive and uneventful. She returned to San Francisco on June 9, 1942, for overhaul and installation of two bow deck torpedo tubes, increasing her total to eight. She resumed service with a new skipper, Commander Thomas Lincoln Wogan who had previously commanded *S-34.* One of Wogan's junior officers was William Robert Anderson, Class of 1943, but graduated June 1942 under the accelerated wartime program. He was fresh from sub school, which had been reduced in length to only three months. Anderson later gained fame by guiding the nuclear-powered submarine *Nautilus* beneath the Arctic ice cap.

Wogan's first patrol on *Tarpon,* her fifth, did nothing to contribute to her glory, nor to his. He was criticized for failing to take full advantage of a great opportunity against a convoy of ten ships and three destroyer escorts. Torpedoes were fired, but none found its mark.

It was the sixth patrol that established *Tarpon's* reputation. Wogan was determined to erase the stigma of his first patrol by coming in with meaningful results. A severe gale that kept *Tarpon* at 120 feet almost thwarted that resolve. However, when the storm abated he found the 10,935-ton passenger-cargo vessel *Fushima Maru,* and sent her to the bottom with three hits out of six fired. He followed that a week later, sinking the huge 16,975-ton passenger liner *Tatsuta Maru,* the third largest Japanese merchantman to be sunk during the war, loaded with troops en route to Truk. These two sinkings catapulted *Tarpon's* record from zero to 29,710 tons confirmed sunk, the best for a single patrol in the war to date.

Tarpon's only action on her seventh patrol was to bombard the Taroa radio station with her deck gun on May 9, 1943. She pumped 49 rounds of 3-inch shells into the target and withdrew before opposition developed. The patrol ended at Pearl Harbor on May 15 for one and a half months of overhaul and training.

On her eighth patrol, *Tarpon* damaged two cargo ships with six torpedoes, but they were not sunk. Another freighter was severely damaged as it left Mikura Shima on August 28, and a 1,000-ton Japanese patrol vessel was sunk on September 4, with all hands lost.

The ninth patrol was off the coast of Honshu from October 1 to November 3, with morale-boosting results. Midway through the patrol a ship was sighted at the approaches to Yokohama. The submarine attacked what Commander Wogan took to be a large naval auxiliary. He fired a spread of four torpedoes, two of which hit the target. Although severely damaged, the enemy ship headed straight for *Tarpon,* the submarine

Bow and stern views of Tarpon. *Note the two torpedo tubes added to the submarine's bow.* (Photo courtesy of the National Archives.)

submerged, went under the vessel and attacked from the other side. Wogan fired two more torpedoes, both of which missed. The enemy ship then fired on *Tarpon,* using everything from machine guns to 6-inch guns. Wogan fired another torpedo. The "up the kilt" shot hit the target's narrow stern. The enemy warship was dead in the water, but she remained afloat. Circling around to the port side of the stationary enemy ship, Wogan fired one more torpedo, and the ship started to sink. Post war examination of enemy records revealed that the ship was German, not Japanese. It proved to be the German raider *Michel* (Shiff-*28*), which had been preying on Allied shipping in both the Atlantic and the Pacific. It was the first German raider sunk in the Pacific by a U.S. submarine, and the last of her kind still afloat at that time. Four days later an aircraft carrier came within range, but four torpedoes missed. Four torpedoes fired at an enemy freighter on October 23 also missed.

The same pattern followed on *Tarpon*'s tenth patrol, with Lieutenant Commander T.B. Oakley in command. Two torpedoes missed an enemy tanker. Six missed the largest ship of a Japanese convoy on the eleventh patrol, commanded by another new skipper, Lieutenant Commander S. Felepone. However, the target was severely damaged by *Tarpon's* deck gun. Three escort vessels were also damaged. The question that had plagued American submarines since the outbreak of the war was "Are the torpedoes defective or are we lousy shots?" The high-technology magnetic-influence exploder torpedoes that the United States had depended upon when the war began had proven worthless. That faulty concept is described more fully in the sinking of U.S. submarine *L-8,* the test target for the magnetic-influence exploder (see Chapter 3). For whatever reason, *Tarpon* had missed golden opportunities with her torpedoes.

Tarpon's last patrol was limited to lifeguard duty rescuing downed airmen in the Truk area. Twelve patrols is a long life for a wartime submarine and *Tarpon* had served her country well, averaging 40 days per patrol, 482 days in all. The submarine was retired from the Pacific Fleet on December 24, 1944. She arrived at New London, Connecticut on January 17, 1945.

After operating on the east coast, *Tarpon* was decommissioned at Boston on November 15, 1945. She served until September 5, 1956 as a Naval Reserve Training Ship for the 8th Naval District in New Orleans. At the end of that service she was struck from the Navy list.

On August 26, 1957, while under tow to Baltimore, Maryland for scrapping, the 22-year-old submarine sank in about 145 feet of water approximately 22 miles from Okracoke Inlet, Cape Hatteras, North Carolina, "graveyard of the Atlantic." The captain of the towing tug boat *Julia C. Moran,* kept the tow line on the sinking submarine until it came to rest on the bottom. He placed a buoy over the spot, although it was unlikely that

Tarpon's periscope frames a Japanese merchant ship off Kwajalein Atoll, Marshall Islands (left). The grid markings aided range calculation. In this instance, the submarine could not get into position for attack. The photo on the right is of the coastline terrain and Japanese installations on Wotje Island, Marshall Islands. Both photos were taken on Tarpon's 10th patrol. (Photos courtesy of the Submarine Force Library and Museum.)

any attempt would be made to raise her. *Tarpon* remained where she was. The decorated World War II submarine was not to submit to the humiliation of being dismantled for scrap in a marine junkyard. Like her namesake, the fighting gamefish, U.S.S. *Tarpon* (SS-*175*) resisted to the end the determined efforts of man to remove her from her element. She ended her days close to the shore of the country she had served so well, where she had enjoyed her greatest triumphs—under the sea.

Diving *Tarpon*

The buoy over *Tarpon's* final resting place disappeared with time. Her exact location remained unknown for more than 25 years. But the remains of many shipwrecks, some hundreds of years old, litter the waters off the North Carolina coast between Cape Hatteras and Cape Fear. And where there are shipwrecks at depths of 250 feet or less, there will be sport divers probing their remains for relics and photographs. The warm clear waters of the Gulf Stream current add to the area's appeal as a Mecca for scuba

Members of Tarpon's *crew on the bridge aft of the conning tower, returning to the New London Submarine Base on January 20, 1945. Lieutenant Commander Richardson, commanding officer, is third from the left.* (Photo courtesy of the Submarine Force Library and Museum.)

divers. Dive-charter boats operate from ports along the North Carolina coast to accommodate them.

In August 1983, dive-charter boat captain Al Wadsworth carried a group of divers, headed for the World War I wreck of the passenger freighter *Proteus*. The 4,836-ton vessel was sunk off Cape Hatteras on the night of August 19, 1918 in a collision with the tanker *Cushing*. *Proteus* had been operating without lights to reduce the possibility of being spotted by German U-boats known to be prowling the area. Gary Gentile, a Philadelphia author and lecturer with extensive diving experience that included the *Andrea Doria,* was aboard. He had heard so much about the remains of the 406-foot long *Proteus* that he was anxious to dive the wreck. It was no wonder that he was less than thrilled by a proposal made by the captain while the charter was still en route to the dive site. Captain Wadsworth had a set of Loran numbers within a mile of *Proteus* that he felt might be anything from a rock pile to a previously undiscovered wreck. He wanted to verify the object, but he was not a diver. He asked Gary to make a quick dive, a bounce off the bottom, to find out what it was before going on to *Proteus*.

Tarpon's bow is broken and angled to the right. Apparently, she hit the bottom bow first and the streamlining exterior hull, forward of the arrow, split off. (The diagram, before the arrow was added, was taken from The Fleet Submarine in the U.S. Navy *by Commander John D. Alden, USN (Ret.), copyright 1979, U.S. Naval Institute; printed by permission.)*

Gentile groaned at the thought of losing precious bottom time that would have to be subtracted from the *Proteus* dive. He had sacrificed good dives before to check out promising leads that turned out to be sand dunes, rock piles, junk heaps, and barges. Still, this could be the exception, and no diver wants to pass up a chance to discover a new wreck. He agreed.

Wadsworth positioned the charter boat over the site with his depth recorder registering an object more than 20 feet high in over 140 feet of water. Gary Gentile and another diver, Bill Nagle, suited up with the temperature well into the nineties. Both hoped for as brief a dive as possible if it was to be unrewarding. But on the chance that it proved worthwhile, Gentile told the captain, "If we're not up in 10 minutes, it means we've found something good."

The divers followed the grapple line to the bottom, Nagle leading. Before he wrapped the chain on a piece of steel projecting from the wreck to secure it, he turned to Gentile with a triumphant grin. Gentile realized that he was looking at the conning tower of a submarine, its periscope housing protruding above like the booms of a fishing trawler. A bronze radar antennae mounted on a thick steel mast loomed aft. The wreck lay heeled over about 30° to port. The divers' self-imposed time limit came and passed as the two examined their find with wonder and exhilaration. The anti-aircraft gun mount was intact with wheels and gears still in place. Only the twin barrels had been removed. All hatches were dogged down and locked from the outside, thoroughly sealing the submarine from entry. Most puzzling was the absence of the submarine's screw-propellers.

When Nagle found a small porthole in the bridge wreckage, Gentile realized they must be on a pre-World War II American submarine. German U-boats never had portholes and U.S. submarines built during World War II had solid coamings to withstand the shock of detonating depth charges. A second porthole and the 100-pound brass gyro-compass lay in the sand.

Gentile and Nagle sent up lift bags with their artifacts attached, then ended their dive. The other divers aboard had realized by then that the dive was indeed worthwhile. They streamed down the grapple line in anticipation, and were not disappointed. There are few experiences in the life of a sport diver to compare with being in the first group to hit a newly discovered wreck and its many historical artifacts.

Gary Gentile's enthusiasm is reflected in his report of the discovery to us on August 24, 1983: "NEWS FLASH!!! I was just diving off of North Carolina, and the captain asked if we would mind checking out a new wreck he had. . . Imagine our surprise when we descended upon the conning tower of a submarine. We recovered two portholes, thus determining that it was an American sub. We also recovered the gyrocompass repeater. . . I've already started researching it. I thought you might be interested, for your book."

Gentile's description of the wreck drew an exclamation from Captain Wadsworth, "This must be the long lost *Tarpon*. They've been looking for it for ten years. But it's supposed to be ten miles from here." It was indeed *Tarpon,* her pressure hull intact, deck just below 130 feet, with the sand bottom 10 to 15 feet deeper. Due to the submarine's list and the weight of the periscopes, the conning tower has fallen into the sand. To gain access to the conning tower's interior, divers must drop down to the sand, go alongside the hull and squirm inside. After gaining entry, it is then difficult to squeeze past the housings of the periscopes.

The bow is broken and angled to the right. Apparently, *Tarpon* hit the bottom bow first and the streamlining exterior hull forward of the pressure hull split and is angled to starboard, barely attached to the rest of the wreck. Several hatches have now been opened by divers, but penetration is discouraged by small amounts of diesel fuel leaking from inside. Another deterrent is that some hatches are difficult to penetrate because they open to a five-foot sleeve that extends down into the interior—entry is like dropping through a five-foot cylinder. The wooden decking is gone and much of the outer shell has corroded away, exposing pumps, valves, pipes and machinery.

Brass artifacts and other collectibles such as shark teeth abound. Sand tiger sharks frequent the wreck. On one dive, 30 or more loomed over the wreck, some of them 14 feet long. They have never bothered anyone, and often depart after divers arrive at the site. Some divers prefer to hover the wreck just to observe the sharks, and perhaps to keep some distance from them despite the docile reputation the sharks have earned. The wreckage is covered with calcareous growth, but little crustaceous marine life.

The wreck lies 22 miles from Okracoke Inlet on a heading of 147°, and 25 miles from Hatteras Inlet on a heading of 183°. It is about four tenths of a mile from the wreck of *Proteus,* with similar diving conditions. Visibility ranges from 30 to 70 feet. Surface current may run up to two knots, but under such conditions there has been little current on the wreck itself. During summer months the water temperature is in the upper 70's to

Open hatches allow divers to penetrate Tarpon's *interior.* (Photo by Brian Skerry.)

mid-80's. Wet suits might not be required, except to provide protection against the calcareous growth.

This dive should be made only by experienced wreck divers who have experience diving far from shore, at the 145-foot depth, and in strong currents.

CHAPTER 10

Dragonet— **Deep, Dark, and Dirty**

Location: upper Chesapeake Bay
Approximate depth of water: 146-154 feet
Visibility: very poor
Current: strong, dive at slack tide
Access: boat

World War II introduced a new era of sophistication in weapons and delivery systems. Powerful torpedoes, depth charges, and sensitive mines were all designed to provide greater effectiveness against enemy targets. A direct hit was not essential to put a vessel out of action. Close exposure to a near contact explosion could rupture the hull of a ship, cause immediate flooding, and put her out of action. Delicate electronic equipment, propulsion systems, and weapons could be damaged to the point where they were useless.

The explosion resistance of hull designs was studied by the Bureau of Ships, using large-scale models or obsolete submarines in their tests. Systems to be evaluated were installed on test targets that were then subjected to explosions. The collected data then guided the development of structural systems to better protect submarines from depth charge attack.

117

Dragonet (SS-*293*) was to play a role in such testing. She was built at the William Cramp and Sons Shipbuilding Company, Philadelphia. The firm had gone out of business in 1926 after building many cruisers and other warships, but *G-4* was its only submarine. The boat was constructed from an Italian design, and its unsatisfactory performance did nothing to enhance Cramp's image.

In 1940, after war erupted in Europe, a group of Philadelphia businessmen purchased the Cramp yard, hoping for defense contracts. The new owners had little shipbuilding experience, but it is reported that President Franklin D. Roosevelt had confidence in their competence. They were assigned orders for many new naval vessels. After the Japanese attack on Pearl Harbor, the Bureau of Ships granted Cramp a contract for 12 submarines even though the company had only one employee with prior submarine experience, Carlton Shugg.

The Cramp yard elected to build their first submarine under the new contract, using a high-tensile steel that the Navy's Portsmouth yard was then developing for use in the heavy-hull design. The design name stemmed from the greater weight of the new steel compared to the mild steel then in use. The extra hull strength it provided would increase a boat's operating depth.

Two months after *Dragonet*'s keel was laid in April 1942, the keel of *Balao,* another heavy-hull submarine, was laid at the Portsmouth Navy Yard. *Balao* was commissioned in seven months; *Dragonet* took two years. As a result, the new class of submarine was named *Balao*.

Cramp had trouble finding skilled labor, probably the reason for the company's many production problems. Those difficulties were multiplied by the resignation of Shugg, the yard's only employee with prior submarine experience. He had repeatedly disagreed with many management decisions before he left. After the war, Shugg joined the Electric Boat Company as general manager.

A major problem arose in building *Dragonet* of trying to make effective welds to the high-tensile steel in her hull. She became notorious for her frequent weld cracks. That makes it surprising that she later withstood depth charge tests as well as she did.

The submarine was 311 feet 8 inches in length, with a beam of 27 feet 3 inches, displacing 1,526 tons when surfaced and 2,314 tons submerged. Her diesel engines could produce a speed of 20 knots on the surface, and her electric motors could move her at almost 9 knots submerged. Her armament was 10 torpedo tubes (6 forward, 4 aft), one 4-inch and one 5-inch deck gun, one 40-mm anti-aircraft gun, and two .50 caliber machine guns. She had a complement of 6 officers and 60 enlisted men.

Fleet submarines such as *Dragonet* were designed with the speed and endurance needed to operate with the battle fleet. They were all named for fish, and were built to cope with an aggressive enemy, as well as the hazards

Dragonet at the Camp Shipbuilding Co., on March 14, 1944. The submarine was sunk in upper Chesapeake Bay by the Underwater Explosive Research Division to develop protective techniques for strengthening the hulls of submarines. (Photo courtesy of the National Archives.)

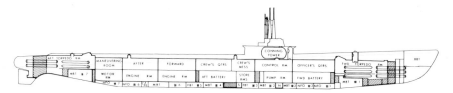

Dragonet and Blenny *were two of 195* Balao-*class submarines completed. There were slight differences in size and displacement among the submarines built at various yards. (The diagram was taken from* The Fleet Submarine in the U.S. Navy *by Commander John D. Alden, USN (Ret.), copyright 1979, U.S. Naval Institute; printed by permission.)*

and long-range logistic problems of operating across the broad Pacific Ocean. Many of their crewmen received their schooling in the smaller and older S-class boats.

Testing

Dragonet was finally commissioned into the Navy on March 6, 1944. The new submarine sailed directly to the New London Submarine Base to serve as a target for depth charge tests. A submarine officer on the staff of the chief of naval operations had offered a radical proposal to the Bureau of Ships in 1940. He convinced the Bureau that brand new submarines be subjected to depth charging with crews on board to test the newest offensive weapon technology against the latest construction design.

Measurements of actual weapons against actual targets, particularly new ones, provided dependable data to determine both weapon effectiveness and the structural changes needed to protect submarines against such weapons. One particularly valuable product of such testing was to establish the minimum amount of explosive required, and the best location near the hull for detonation to ensure crippling of the target vessel.

The first target to be tested was *Tambor* (SS-*198*). Her commanding officer, Lieutenant Commander John N. Murphey, Jr., was less than pleased at the prospect that his command and her entire crew might be killed by the concussion. The antiquated submarine *G-2,* had served as a depth charge test target in 1919, but her crew was not on board when the explosives were detonated.

For *Tambor's* test, an explosive charge of 300 pounds of TNT was moored at the submarine's periscope depth. A submarine rescue vessel, anchored about a half mile away, fired the charge as the submarine cruised past, 500 yards from the explosive charge. The effect, as reported to the Bureau of Ships, was ". . . a sensation similar to slamming a watertight door . . . sharp, metallic jolt. Not very intense."

The submarine then made a pass at 340 yards. The result was a louder noise, considerable vibration, and lateral displacement of the boat. A third test at 275 yards produced minor damage and a fuel-oil leak. The crew was then removed and the boat was moored only 100 feet from the next detonation. Many instruments were damaged, but the hull was not breached. Such tests guided the Bureau of Ships in its material development programs.

In *Dragonet's* test, the new submarine was moored, without her crew, only 75 feet from the explosive charge. The surprise was that only minor damage resulted. It had been expected that her construction problem of deficient welding would have left her subject to more severe damage under the rigors of the test.

War Duty

After completing the test, welding cracks that had developed were repaired and *Dragonet* left New London for Pearl Harbor; she arrived there on October 9, 1944. Her first war patrol on November 1, was to the Kurile Islands and the Sea of Okohotsk. She was traveling submerged when she struck an uncharted, underwater peak; it caved in and holed her pressure hull in the forward torpedo room. Seawater poured through, and the space instantly flooded, plummeting the boat out of control, toward crush depth.

(text continued on page 129)

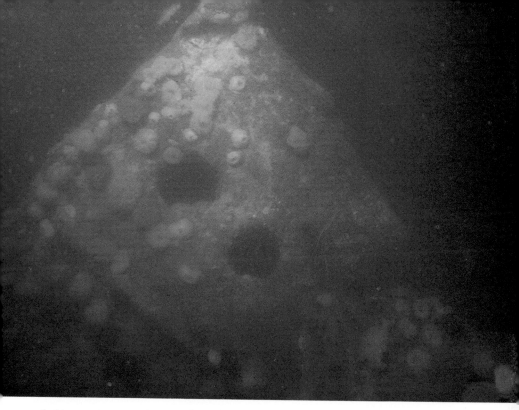

L-8's *conning tower's streamlined housing has separated from the pressure hull.* (Photo by Bill Campbell.)

L-8's *open conning tower hatch.* (Photo by Bill Campbell.)

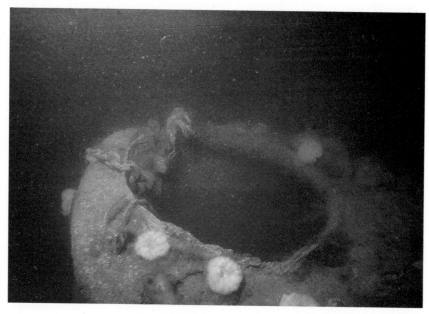

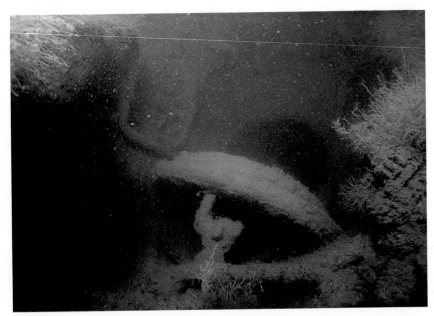

Inside L-8's *conning tower. The open hatch leads down to the control room.* (Photo by Bill Campbell.)

An external control wheel on L-8's *pressure hull is almost completely surrounded by sea anemones and hydrozoans.* (Photo by Bill Campbell.)

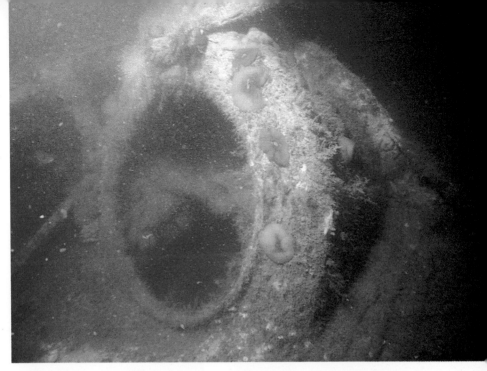

L-8's torpedo loading hatch opens into the torpedo room. (Photo by Bill Campbell.)

Scattered debris and equipment inside L-8. (Photo by Bill Campbell.)

◀ *Two control wheels inside* L-8, *forward of the control room.* (Photo by Bill Campbell.)

▼ *Looking aft over a solid bronze torpedo tube in* L-8's *forward torpedo room. This tube was recovered by Bill Palmer.* (Photo by Bill Campbell.)

▼ *An unconscious survivor of the* S-5 *disaster is evacuated. The steel plate cut from the submarine's stern to release the trapped men is now on display in the Navy Museum at the Washington Navy Yard.* (Painting by Otto von Fisher, courtesy of the Submarine Force Library and Museum.)

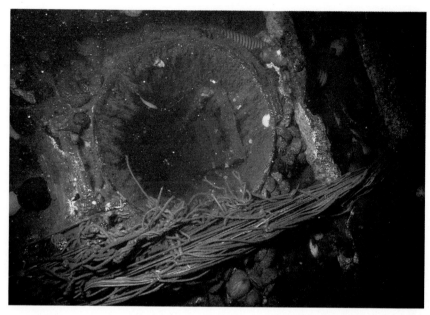

An open hatch on S-5 invites inspection. (Photo by Gary Gentile.)

S-5's conning tower. (Photo by Gary Gentile.)

A diver takes his position on S-16's one-man "chariot bridge," the uppermost part of the conning tower. The name stems from its two-tier silhouette. (Photo by Gary Gentile.)

S-5's anemone covered screw-propeller. (Photo by Gary Gentile.)

S-16 *air induction valve at the base of the conning tower. A rescue diver could attach an air line to the connection, at left center, to pump air to trapped submariners. The valve's control wheel can be seen in the center. The induction valve was an improvement that was added to S boats after* S-5 *sank.* (Photo by Gary Gentile.)

▶ *A telegraph recovered from* S-16 *by Billy Deans of Key West Diver, Inc.* (Photo by H. Keatts.)

▼ *A diver inspects one of* S-16's *running lights at the base of the conning tower.* (Photo by Gary Gentile.)

Inside S-49's *conning tower, with a speaking tube (on the right) adapted for use as a conduit for wiring from the control room below. The jerryrigged change was made during her use as a test platform. A torpedo firing switch is on the left.* (Photo by Gary Gentile.)

S-49 *capstan cover.* (Photo by Gary Gentile.)

(text continued from page 120)

The crew quickly reacted, expelling the water from all forward ballast and trim tanks and much of the water from the torpedo room. That provided just enough positive buoyancy for the submarine to reach the surface. She broke through—directly in front of a Japanese gun emplacement, just four miles from Matsuwa's airfield. Either the gun was unmanned, or the gun crew was asleep. *Dragonet* was unchallenged as she quickly cleared the danger area.

The grounding had damaged the submarine's bow planes, and the only way to rerig them was from inside the flooded compartment. The following day compressed air was released into the forward battery room and the ruptured torpedo room. The watertight door between them was opened and, with the submarine's electrical system fully exposed to flooding if the sea should break through, crewmen made the repairs. They succeeded, but before the boat arrived at Midway on December 20, two days of storms almost sent her to the bottom.

After emergency repairs, *Dragonet* went to Mare Island for overhaul. She returned to Pearl Harbor on April 2, 1945, and two weeks later left on her second war patrol. The submarine was stationed south of the Japanese home islands for lifeguard duty, to rescue downed aviators. Four Army airmen were recovered from the sea during the non-aggressive patrol.

Between June 10 and July 8, *Dragonet* was refitted at Guam for her final war patrol. It was an aggressive mission, but she was also to be prepared to save downed airmen in the area of Bungo Suido. It was late in the war, and U.S. submarines had already decimated the Japanese merchant fleet. There were no contacts with enemy vessels, but one naval airman was rescued.

When the war ended, *Dragonet* put into Saipan, then sailed to Pearl Harbor and San Francisco. She was rewarded for her second and third patrols with two battle stars. On April 16, 1946 the submarine, still only two years old, was decommissioned and placed in reserve at Mare Island, San Francisco. During that year, the Underwater Explosions Research Division (UERD) was established by the Navy. It was charged with the diverse objectives of developing protective technology to strengthen ship and submarine hulls, and providing guidance to improve underwater weapons performance.

In 1961, *Dragonet* was sent to Portsmouth, Virginia, where UERD made her fully operational. She was then subjected to what was described as "mix-master" testing—repeated rapid submerging, surfacing, and rocking from side to side by remote control of water ballast. The "shaking up" was intended to expose areas for improving explosion shock resistance in the Navy's future underwater fleet. In her final test, *Dragonet* was intentionally sunk by an explosion, near Hooper Island, in upper Chesapeake Bay.

Diving *Dragonet*

Ed Suarez, an experienced wreck diver from Columbia, Maryland, had learned of a U.S. Navy submarine lying in 150 feet of water, near Hooper Island. His research suggested that it might be *Dragonet*. He enlisted the help of a friend, Mike Moore, also an experienced wreck diver, who owned a trailerable boat that could take them to the site. The two checked a nautical chart of upper Chesapeake Bay, and found only one Hooper Island area location with the reported depth of the submarine. It was Anderson Deep.

Suarez and Moore launched a search for the submarine in June, 1987, 26 years after her sinking. A few quick passes with the depth sounder defined Anderson Deep, less than one mile long and only a few hundred yards wide. However, a full day of searching with depth sounder and scanning sonar revealed nothing. Discouraged, the two divers headed home, disappointed but still determined.

Additional research confirmed the earlier findings through the Automated Wreck and Obstruction Information System (AWOIS), a computer data bank maintained by the National Oceanographic and Atmospheric Administration. It gave the name of the submarine, its history, and the latitude and longitude of her position. Reference to the nautical charts confirmed that position to be Anderson Deep.

In May 1988, another veteran wreck diver, Uwe Lovas from Stafford, Virginia, searched for *Dragonet* and other wrecks in the area. Lovas, using a paper recording fathometer, located the submarine in 154 feet of water, lying in an east-west direction, within 150 yards of the documented sinking location. The Loran C numbers he gave the authors are 27446.0, 42250.6, and 58811.8. The wreck lies in the ship channel and Lovas had to move out of the way of freighters on two occasions during his search. He did not dive the wreck because of the strong current and ship traffic.

The following year Suarez requested the Loran numbers from Lovas. He and Moore returned to Anderson Deep in April 1989, and made a second attempt to find *Dragonet*. Several hours of searching with the depth sounder revealed nothing until a faint echo was recorded. The divers reasoned that a 1,526-ton submarine should have produced a much stronger signal, but the 146-foot depth was close to the reported depth. They decided to hook the potential object and dive to identify it.

Suarez made one dive and Moore dove twice into a very strong current and only three-foot visibility. Mostly by touch, they found the elusive submarine, buried in mud almost to her deck, accounting for the poor printout of the depth recorder. Suarez later described the dive as "a descent into the pit of hell."

Dragonet is a Balao-*class submarine.* (Illustration by James L. Christley.)

Moore reported that *Dragonet* lies in Anderson Deep, near the Hooper Straits (Loran numbers for the stern are 27446.1 and 42250.5), in 146 feet of water, her main deck at about 141 feet, the top of the conning tower about 95 feet. The nearest launching ramp is at Merkins Neck on the eastern shore, but the best and most convenient ramp for most people is run by the state. It is on the north side of the Patuxent River where Route 4 crosses at Solomons, Maryland, about seven nautical miles across the Bay from the wreck.

Mike Moore has warned that *Dragonet* is a difficult dive. The depth is beyond commonly accepted sport diving limits, there is no light down there, and the visibility is typical of Chesapeake Bay (poor). Most of the hull has settled into the soft silt bottom, which is easily stirred up by fin kicks. There is not much small boat traffic in that part of the Bay, but large ships and current can still be problems. All of the precautions for hazardous diving apply: multiple lights, multiple decompression plans, and maybe even a search line attached to the anchor.

Moore claims that for a "sub-freak," *Dragonet* is worth the attempt. She is one of the few sunken submarines that is at a diveable depth, her hull is intact, she is untouched and holds great promise for those who are willing and capable of reaching her deep, dark, and dirty resting place.

CHAPTER 11

Blenny—
Celebrated Artificial Reef

Location: 12 miles south-southeast of Ocean City Inlet, Maryland
Approximate depth of water: 70 feet
Visibility: averages about 15 feet
Current: little
Access: boat

The operating depth of the *Balao*-class fleet submarines of World War II was one of the best-kept secrets of the war. The diving depth of the previous *Gato*-class was 300 feet. The operating depth of the new class was increased to 400 feet by using high-tensile steel instead of mild steel, and increasing the thickness of the pressure-hull plating. *Balao*-class boats became known as "thick skins"; the *Gato*-class submarines were called "thin skins."

The new pressure-hull plate was 7/8-inch thick and weighed 35 pounds per square foot compared to 27.5-pound, 9/16-inch plate in the previous class. On paper the new hulls should have withstood submergence to 925 feet without collapsing. However, tests showed that some of the vital machinery could not function at even close to that depth. The trim pump, for example, could not develop the required discharge pressure. Thus the operating depth of the new boats was set at 400 feet, but the test requirements for internal machinery was one and a half times the pressure of 450 feet, a substantial safety margin. That proved to be fortunate when government specifications for high-tensile steel were relaxed. The steel that originally was chrome-vanadium, with a yield strength of 50,000 pounds per square inch, was changed to a titanium-manganese alloy with a 45,000 p.s.i. yield strength. The new specifications were still considerably stronger than mild steel with the extra margin of safety, the operating depth remained at 400 feet.

External and internal appearances of both classes of boats were essentially identical leaving the Japanese unaware of the increased operating depth. The older Japanese RO-class submarines could dive to only 150 feet, a fragility that tended to be fatal under a depth-charge attack. The newer I-class Japanese boats had an operating depth of 300 feet. Their hulls, however, were not as strong as either the American *Gato-* or *Balao*-class boats.

Blenny (SS-*324*) was one of 195 *Balao*-class boats that were completed. There were slight differences of size and displacement, depending upon which of the yards built the submarines. *Blenny* was 311 feet 9 inches long and her beam was 27 feet 3 inches. She displaced 1,526 tons on the surface and 2,424 tons submerged. Her diesels produced about 20 knots on the surface; electric motors propelled her at almost 9 knots while submerged. Armament consisted of 10 torpedo tubes (6 forward and 4 aft), 24 torpedoes, one 5-inch deck gun, one 40-mm and one 20-mm anti-aircraft gun, and two .50 caliber machine guns. The boat had a complement of 6 officers and 60 enlisted men.

She was built by the Electric Boat Company at Groton, Connecticut, the 62nd submarine to be built by the company during World War II. After commissioning on July 27, 1944 with Lieutenant Commander W.H. Hazzard in command, she conducted preliminary torpedo firing training until she left for Key West, Florida, on August 29. She underwent a short training period at the Sonar School, then left for Balboa, Panama Canal Zone, where she arrived on September 19. After another short but intensive training period, *Blenny* reported to the Pacific Fleet at Pearl Harbor on October 15.

War Service

Although she only saw action from November 1944 to August 1945, *Blenny* was awarded four battle stars for four successful war patrols in the Java and South China Seas. She used torpedoes, gunfire, and boarding parties with demolition charges to sink 80 Japanese vessels totaling over 43,000 tons. Four ships, totaling almost 25,000 tons, were damaged.

On her first war patrol *Blenny* missed a Japanese destroyer with one torpedo, and was heavily depth charged in return. She then sank an

Blenny's *World War II crew with her commanding officer Lieutenant Commander Hazzard in the center of the second row. He commanded the submarine through-out the war.* (Photo courtesy of the Submarine Force Library and Museum.)

800-ton destroyer escort with two torpedoes and in a surface attack torpedoed a 10,000-ton transport, *Kenzui Maru,* loaded with troops. A 4,000-ton cargo ship was severely damaged with one torpedo, and a small naval patrol vessel was sunk by gunfire. *Blenny* narrowly escaped destruction in an aerial attack by Japanese antisubmarine patrol.

During her second war patrol, she torpedoed and sank the 10,200-ton tanker *Amato Maru* in a submerged moonlight attack, and damaged two of the same class. Three weeks later she sank three freighters, totaling 15,750 tons, and her gunfire sank a small fishing vessel.

Her third patrol was divided between hunting for enemy vessels and lifeguard duty for aviators downed at sea. She torpedoed the sub chaser *Kairyu* off the north coast of Java in a night surface attack. The extremely shallow water made it a remarkable attack against the target, which was anchored close in to the beach. To get at her, *Blenny*, backed in toward the beach, taking soundings from the stern with a lead line. At the time of firing, the submarine was in 25 feet of water with her screws stirring up silt. Five days later she added the freighter *Hokoku Maru* and the minesweeper *105* to her list of victims.

Blenny's fourth and final patrol of the war added a large number of sampans, junks and miscellaneous small craft to her record. They were sunk after preliminary inspection, to determine that they were carrying contraband, and after seeing the crews safely clear. Several of the vessels were sunk with a 12-gauge shotgun that was fired through the bottom of the captured vessel from the inside. A large naval gunboat and a freighter were also sunk.

During the patrol, the U.S. submarine *Cod* (SS-*224*) intercepted a large three-masted junk and put a six-man boarding party aboard. The junk was transporting contraband to Singapore, which was still occupied by the Japanese. Before *Cod*'s boarding party could sink the junk and return to the submarine, a Japanese fighter plane arrived and strafed both vessels. *Cod* dove amid a hail of machine gun slugs. The enemy plane stayed in the area until a Japanese warship arrived. That prevented the submarine from surfacing to check on the boarding crew.

Cod's radio report of the action was received by four U.S. submarines in the vicinity. The four, including *Blenny*, joined the search for the missing submariners. Two days later, when the search seemed hopeless, *Blenny*'s crew sighted a junk that matched the description given by *Cod*'s commander. When the submarine pulled alongside, the entire boarding party was found on board, receiving good treatment from the Chinese crew. The junk was spared and her crew were presented with gifts of canned goods and fresh bread. *Cod*'s rescued crewmen returned to their submarine, to a jubilant welcome from their fellow crew members.

Between World War II and the Korean conflict *Blenny* operated off the U.S. Pacific coast, except for a cruise to China in 1946 and fleet maneuvers off Hawaii in 1950. In 1951, her hull was streamlined, and she was modernized and converted into a *Guppy*-class submarine. The streamlining and diesel-electric direct drive engines increased her speed to 15 knots. Additional bow and stern torpedo tubes were installed along with higher-capacity batteries. Surface displacement was increased by over 300 tons, but her length was shortened by almost five feet by rounding the bow. Most of the *Balao*-class submarines were converted in this manner, and made up the bulk of the Navy's submarine force until they were replaced by nuclear-powered attack submarines in the 1960s.

Between May and November 1952, the submarine operated in the Far East, including a 35-day reconnaissance patrol in support of operations in Korea. *Blenny* received her fifth and final battle star for that mission. She returned to the West Coast and remained there until she reported to the Atlantic Fleet on May 24, 1954, operating out of New London. In 1966, her conning tower fairweather was replaced with a hydrodynamic "sail" made of fiberglass, transparent to both radar and sonar. The hydrophones of the passive ranging sonar equipment, finlike mountings on her deck, were also added.

Three faces of Blenny. *The photo above shows her in her original configuration. The middle photo depicts the boat after her 1951 "Guppy" conversion. The bottom photo shows* Blenny *during the 1960s, showing even more technological advancements in her design during the latter stages of her career.* (Photos courtesy of the Submarine Force Library and Museum.)

Blenny functioned as an experimental boat until she transferred to the inactive fleet at Philadelphia. The diesel-electric submarine, rendered obsolete by nuclear powered vessels, was decommissioned in 1969, stricken from the Navy list in 1973 and moved to Portsmouth, Virginia.

Sinking

In 1978, she was designated as a target to be sunk by the 2nd Fleet. In 1979, the submarine was moved to the Patuxent Naval Air Test Center, near Solomons, Maryland. However, *Blenny* was saved by John Foster of Maryland's Tidewater Administration. His purpose was to "use the ship as a center point of creating an artificial reef. . . to improve fish productivity for sport fishermen."

Foster had been interested in using another submarine for his purpose, not *Blenny*. In 1987, while overseeing the sinking of a barge as an artificial reef, the tow-crew mentioned *Turbot* (SS-*427*), another *Balao*-class boat. World War II had ended before the submarine was completed by the Cramp Shipbuilding Company, construction stopped, and she was launched half-completed as a bare hull. She was never commissioned, but she did have a useful career after being turned over to the Naval Research and Development Center in 1950. The submarine was used for several years as a machinery research and test platform. Noise-reduction features were developed and tested in *Turbot*'s hull. Then, with her usefulness to the Navy over, she sat in Carr Creek, Annapolis, Maryland, falling into disrepair. Foster contacted the Navy and expressed interest in the derelict submarine. However, Senator Claude Pepper (D-Fla.) informed the Navy that his own constituents in Southern Florida wanted that boat for the diving community. *Turbot* was alloted to Florida and Maryland was compensated with *Blenny*, which was sitting at the Patuxant Air Naval Station.

Foster was pleased. *Blenny*, which had been designated as a target, had already been cleaned and prepared for towing. More important, the submarine he had been awarded had five war patrols to her credit and had achieved historical significance. *Turbot* had nothing like that to offer.

Congressman Roy Dyson of Maryland sponsored the legislation and Congress granted the Navy permission to give *Blenny* to the state of Maryland. However, the problem of residual liability arose. The federal government wanted release from liability and a Maryland state law limits the state's financial liability. To break the stalemate, the municipality of Ocean City, Maryland, received title to the submarine.

Tony Barret, Ocean City Manager, stated that, "The main industry in Ocean City is tourism. The addition of the *Blenny* off our coast will be a welcome attraction to sport fishermen and divers."

The Maryland Department of Natural Resources was responsible for the final preparations for sinking the submarine. A salvage company removed her periscopes and two engines from the forward engine room before towing her about 12 nautical miles south-southeast of Ocean City Inlet.

U.S. Army Special Forces and U.S. Navy Seals placed charges of C4 explosive and kerosene within the submarine's hull. Amid flames and smoke, the 45-year-old *Blenny* made her final dive on June 7, 1989. Several explosions forward and aft sank her in about 70 feet of water. Forty-four of her former crew members, including Hazzard and nine others of her original World War II crew, watched from one of several boats in attendance. Rod Farb, author and veteran wreck diver, wrote in *Skin Diver* magazine, "The unanimous consensus among the crew is that this is a fitting resting place for the submarine named for a fish; it is quite fitting she has become a home for other fish."

Flames and smoke rise from Blenny *as she makes her last dive on June 6, 1989. The submarine was sunk as an artificial reef off Ocean City, Maryland.* (Photo courtesy of the Ocean City Department of Public Relations.)

Diving *Blenny*

Mike Moore of Baltimore, Maryland, another veteran wreck diver, first saw *Blenny* in November 1986. He told us, "I found her tied up at the Naval Target Support Group in Solomons. A phone call to the Public Affairs office revealed her history and impending use as a target. The following spring I found her moored out in Chesapeake Bay in a non-target area. Another call revealed that funding had been cut and the Navy had no other place to put her."

About three weeks before the submarine was to be sunk, Moore was asked to check her screw-propellers, shafts and thru-hulls. Diving under her he found "both props and one shaft were gone. . . The next time I saw her was on the end of a towline off Ocean City." He later wrote that ships ". . . die. Some die natural deaths, succumbing to nature's stress. Some are murdered by act of war. And some, mothballed, comatose, are quietly put to sleep."

Blenny was put to sleep, and now lies on her starboard side, her conning tower resting on the sand and her bow facing southwest. The submarine's portside hull is about 50 feet from the surface providing plenty of bottom time. Visibility averages about 15 feet. For easy and safe access by divers, 4 x 8-foot square holes were cut through the deck into both torpedo rooms, both engine rooms, and the forward battery room. To provide for diver safety, hatch covers were chained and locked open. However, as she sank, interior partitions and other materials broke loose. The debris can entangle a diver and caution should be used when penetrating the hull.

Many artifacts have been removed by divers, but many remain for future divers. The Ocean City Lifesaving Museum is preparing an exhibit about the fleet submarine *Blenny* and will display artifacts that have been recovered and donated by divers.

There is an excellent launching ramp in the commercial basin of the harbor. Loran numbers are 27024.1 and 42203.4. Information on dive-boat charters can be obtained from the director of public relations for the town of Ocean City, at (301) 289-2800.

Another interesting dive in the area is the tanker *African Queen* (Loran numbers are 27022.7 and 42202.2) which sank in December 1958, during a treacherous storm. The tanker's bow section is only a couple of hundred yards from the submarine.

CHAPTER 12

Spikefish—The World's "Divingest" Submarine

Location: about 55 miles south of Block Island, Rhode Island, the exact location is unknown
Approximate depth of water: 255 feet
Visibility: probably good
Current: moderate to strong
Access: boat

The *Guinness Book of World Records* is an interesting documentation of notable people, animals, plant life, and other objects. All are noted because they are, or have done something faster, longer, more often, or on a larger scale than others. The tallest, shortest, fastest, strongest, and oldest are all identified, as well as consumers of the most flapjacks, hotdogs, oysters, and bananas. But one record has not received recognition from the book's editors. On March 18, 1960 U.S. Navy submarine *Spikefish* became the first submarine in the world to record 10,000 dives. For some reason, that achievement does not appear in the Guinness pages.

The record setting submarine received appropriate attention from Navy officials and the media when the record was set. She still holds the 10,000-dive record. At the earlier avarage rate of 625 dives per year, her

The Balao-*class fleet submarine* Spikefish *established a world record of 10,000 dives on March 18, 1960.* (Photo courtesy of the Submarine Force Library and Museum.)

lifetime total would have reached 11,875 dives. Most of her record setting dives were made while she was training over 12,000 officers and men at the U.S. Naval Submarine School, New London, Connecticut.

There are many reasons why 10,000 dives by a submarine in 16 years is remarkable:

- It was twice the number by any U.S. submarine in 1960, when it was set.
- The record may never be broken. More modern submarines make fewer dives of longer duration.
- The nuclear powered submarine *Nautilus* would have had to operate until the year 2003 to dive 10,000 times, if she had remained in service beyond her March 8, 1980 decommissioning.
- Each *Spikefish* dive took on 300 tons of seawater, then expelled it to surface. Thus, 6 million displacement tons flowed through her flood valves in setting her record. That amounts to 210 million cubic feet of water.
- Water cascades over Niagara Falls at 212,200 cubic feet a second. At that rate, it would take the mighty Niagara 16 1/2 minutes to flow the same volume of water the record setting submarine moved into and out of her ballast tanks in diving 10,000 times.

Spikefish was named for the fighting striped marlin that frequents the Western Seaboard of the United States. Game fishermen recognize that spectacular fighter from the central figure of the submarine's aggressive emblem patch (page 144). Diving was not the only accomplishment the submarine could claim. She entered service in the waning days of World

War II, but was awarded three battle stars. She was credited with damaging one medium freighter, sinking a small Japanese freighter with her deck gun, and sinking an enemy submarine with two torpedo hits. She also engineered the daring rescue of a downed fighter pilot only five miles from Japanese guns on the coast of Ishigaki.

Spikefish (SS-*404*) was built at the Portsmouth (New Hampshire) Navy yard. She was launched on April 26, 1944, three months after her keel was laid on January 29, 1944. Her sponsor was Mrs. Harvey Wilson Moore, Jr., whose husband, Lieutenant Moore, perished when the submarine *Pickerel* (SS-*177*) was sunk by the Japanese in 1943. *Spikefish* was commissioned on June 30, with Commander N.J. Nicholas in command.

The new submarine was a *Baloa*-class boat, 311 feet 8 inches long, and with a beam of 27 feet 3 inches. Her surfaced displacement was 1,810 tons, submerged 2,415 tons. She was designed for a speed of 20 knots on the surface, 8.75 knots submerged. Armament included ten 21-inch torpedo tubes, one 5-inch deck gun and one 40-mm gun. The new submarine carried a complement of 81 officers and men.

For thirty days *Spikefish* underwent training and shakedown along the New England coast. She returned to Portsmouth for additional work, then left for Panama, where she underwent an additional five days of training in preparation for assignment to the Pacific Fleet; she arrived at Pearl Harbor on October 23, in company with the U.S. submarine *Sea Owl* (SS-*405*).

War Patrols

On November 15, 1944, she left Pearl Harbor on her first war mission. She refueled at Midway, en route to her patrol of the Kuril Islands, which separate the Sea of Okhotsk from the Pacific Ocean, north of Japan. It was an extremely cold and very rough patrol, with no enemy contacts. The cold was so intense that frequent dives were made to thaw out frozen vents. The only vessels sighted were two Russian ships. *Spikefish* ended that uneventful 48-day mission on January 1, 1945 when she arrived back at Midway.

A four-day training period followed routine refitting, and *Spikefish* departed for Guam, then headed for patrol in the Nansei Shoto area of the Ryuku Islands, south of Japan. She arrived on February 11, but made no contact with the enemy for almost two weeks. On February 24, at 8:36 a.m., a convoy of six medium sized freighters protected by four escorts was sighted. The submarine made a submerged attack, firing six torpedoes at two of the freighters from a range of 3,800 yards. Three hits were heard, but the nearest escort forced *Spikefish* to submerge before the results could be assessed. Eighty depth charges were dropped on the submarine throughout the morning. At 12:30 p.m. the attack ceased, and a half hour later

Spikefish surfaced to find nothing in sight. She was credited with damaging one freighter of 5,000 tons.

On March 5, near Akuseki Island, a north-bound convoy was sighted. It included three small freighters, a small tanker, and at least four escorts. Six torpedoes were fired at two of the ships, but they missed. *Spikefish* dove to escape 12 depth charges that did no damage. She returned to Pearl Harbor on March 19, after a 53-day mission, with 24 days spent in the assigned patrol area.

During the stay at Pearl Harbor the submarine underwent routine refit, while her officers and crew enjoyed several weeks of relaxation. On March 24, her commanding officer, Commander N.J. Nicholas, was relieved by Lieutenant Commander R.R. Managhan. Eleven days of training, from April 5, to April 16, readied *Spikefish* for her third war patrol. She arrived at Guam on May 1, in company with the U.S. submarine *Dragonet* (see Chapter 10).

Two days later, *Spikefish* left for patrol station in the Formosa area on what was primarily a lifeguard assignment; nearly all enemy shipping had already been eliminated from those waters. For 20 days the submarine patrolled the east coast of the island, while numerous air strikes were made against Japanese installations. However, no airmen were forced down on her side of the island for the submarine to rescue. Only one enemy vessel was sighted, tentatively identified as a freighter of about 300 tons, but darkness and poor visibility made positive identification impossible. Four torpedoes were fired. All missed the target.

Spikefish was ordered to transfer from the coast of Formosa to Sakishima Gunto as lifeguard for U.S. carrier planes attacking Japanese installations in the area. For the first week of June, the submarine observed many air strikes against the entrenched enemy at close range. She fired 29 rounds of her 5-inch shells during a bombardment of Miyara airstrip on Ishigaki Jima on June 5, 1944. A Japanese radio announcement several days later reported, accurately or not, that only one plane had been affected by the bombardment.

On June 7, the submarine responded to a message that a plane had crash landed southeast of Ishigaki, about 20 miles away. A fighter pilot from the U.S. carrier *Sargent Bay* was rescued from a rubber raft by *Spikefish* about five miles from the coast of Ishigaki. The submarine returned to Guam on June 13, after a patrol of 55 days, 30 of them spent on patrol station.

Two Sinkings

On July 8, *Spikefish* left on her fourth war patrol, once again for a lifeguard station, this time in the vicinity of Nanpo Shoto, south of the Japanese islands. About one week later she headed for the East China Sea on a search for enemy shipping. Chinese craft were numerous, but no Japanese ships were sighted. The most exciting activity was to sink floating mines with rifle fire. The submarine continued her patrol southward in the Shanghai area of the East China Sea. On August 6, a large task force steamed into view. *Spikefish* closed to investigate, but Lieutenant Commander Managhan was unable to exchange satisfactory recognition signals. He finally identified several of the vessels as American destroyers. Without an exchange of signals, *Spikefish* might have been mistaken as an enemy submarine. She was forced to dive, and ran deep and silent as the destroyers passed directly over her. Managhan later reported the harrowing experience as "the dread of destruction by your own side." Five days later, over one month into her patrol, a small Japanese freighter of about 250 tons was sighted and sunk by gunfire. The vessel, referred to as a sea truck, did not warrant the expenditure of a valuable torpedo. Three enemy survivors were taken aboard.

The Japanese were preparing to defend their homeland against invasion. They had lost Iwo Jima and Okinawa, and expected the Allies to strike the home island of Kyushu next. The Japanese high command had correctly guessed which beaches the Allies had chosen for invasion. Japanese propagandists declared that the enemy was being enticed to invade that island so that "samurai" warriors could destroy them "at one stroke." The great Chinese army and armada of Kublai Khan had been destroyed on Kyushu beacheads in A.D. 1280 by fanatic Japanese defenders with the assistance of the legendary "kamikaze" typhoon. Twentieth-century fanatics had prepared 5,350 "kamikaze" planes and 5,000 young pilots. An additional several thousand planes were being repaired for one-way suicide missions. However, the Japanese desperately needed aviation fuel before the "divine wind" could strike. The Japanese high command drew up an ambitious plan to import 2,000,000 gallons of gasoline from Singapore and Formosa.

A cloth patch insignia of Spikefish. (Photo by H. Keatts.)

U.S. submarines had decimated their tanker fleet, and what few remained would probably be sunk if they were used to transport the fuel. As an alternative, several Japanese attack submarines were converted to tankers. After conversion, an I-class boat could transport 182,000 gallons.

On August 9, *I-373,* one of the converted fleet submarines, left Sasebo for Formosa on her first tanker run. On the evening of August 13, *Spikefish* made radar contact with a large surfaced submarine that was zigzagging at ten knots on a southwesterly course. Managhan reported the contact to Rear Admiral Charles Lockwood, Commander Submarines Pacific, and continued to track the vessel until the target detected *Spikefish.* The unidentified submarine suddenly zigged to a northeasterly course, dove, and broke contact. Managhan reasoned that her commander would reverse course immediately after submerging. He followed suit, changing course to a southwesterly direction, and again established contact shortly after midnight. Meanwhile, Lockwood radioed that the contact must be Japanese as *Spikefish* was the only U.S. submarine in the area. *Spikefish* maintained position with the submarine until dawn, when first light revealed a profile that was definitely Japanese. The U.S. submarine closed and fired six torpedoes at a range of 1,300 yards. Two hits sank the Japanese submarine stern first in a large cloud of smoke. Five Japanese survivors, remained in the water feigning death. None would board *Spikefish* until one was forcibly hauled aboard. The Japanese vessel was identified as *I-373* (1,660 tons).

World War II ended the following day. *Spikefish* had sunk the 127th, and last, submarine lost by Japan in the war. *I-373* was sacrificed in a cause that was already lost. Earlier acceptance of the inevitable by the Japanese might have saved the submarine and her crew. The submarine had left Sasebo three days after the first atomic bomb hit Hiroshima, and the same day an atomic bomb devastated Nagasaki.

Hostilities were at an end. *Spikefish* put in at Tanapang Harbor, Saipan on August 21, and transferred her prisoners. The next day she departed for Pearl Harbor, spent one week there, then headed for the east coast of the United States in company with the U.S. submarine *Hoe* (SS-*258*). She arrived at the New London submarine base on September 29. After participating in a Navy Day celebration at Charleston, South Carolina, she returned to the Portsmouth Navy Yard for a three and a half month overhaul that was completed February 15, 1946.

Training Vessel

For the next nine years, until April 1955, *Spikefish* alternated the training of officers and men at the New London Submarine Training School with attack exercises, training cruises, exercises with aircraft and

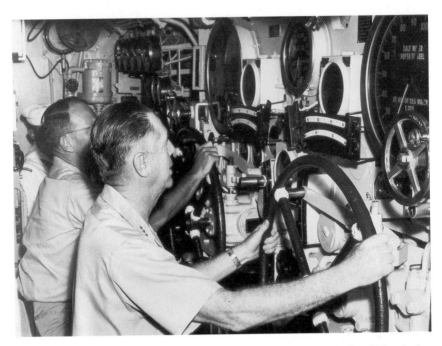

On the occasion of the 10,000th dive of Spikefish, *Rear Admiral Lloyd Mustin (on the left), Commander Key West Submarine Force, and Vice Admiral Fitzhugh Lee, Deputy Commander in Chief, U.S. Atlantic Fleet, man the dive plane controls. This dive made* Spikefish *the "divingest submarine in the world."* (Photo courtesy of the Submarine Force Library and Museum.)

periods of overhaul. She conducted a series of three-day training cruises for reserve midshipmen in Guantanamo Bay, and made periodic cruises to the Caribbean for Atlantic Fleet maneuvers. Exercises with various patrol squadrons of aircraft were held off the Virginia Capes and at Jacksonville and Key West, Florida. Her overhaul periods were spent at the Portsmouth, Philadelphia and Charleston Naval Shipyards.

In August and September 1955, *Spikefish* joined units of the Sixth Fleet at Phaeleron Bay, Greece, for exercises with the British submarine *Trenchant* and combined maneuvers with units of the Royal Hellenic Navy in the area of Suda Bay, Crete. Then came a schedule of training maneuvers in the Malta area. She cleared Gibraltar on September 26, en route back to New London, where she arrived on October 8, 1955.

Her next eight years were spent in training duties and maneuvers in local operating areas, along the Eastern Seaboard and the Caribbean. She also made practice cruises to Halifax, Nova Scotia, and performed service for the Fleet Sonar School, Key West, Florida.

World Record

Spikefish received her most lasting tribute on March 18, 1960, when she became the first submarine of any navy to record 10,000 dives. It is a record that is not likely to be bettered, except by her own accumulation of additional dives before her decommissioning on April 2, 1963.

The 19-year-old submarine received three battle stars for her World War II service, sank the last Japanese submarine to be sunk during the war, and established a remarkable world record for diving. She had served her country well, but her time was past. She was struck from the Navy list on May 1, 1963, and was subsequently sunk as a target off the coast of Long Island, New York on August 4, 1964.

Diving *Spikefish*

We know of no commercial divers or sport divers who have searched for this historic submarine. More than ten years ago we obtained Loran A numbers (1952 and 5490) for what was believed to be the wreck site. An old nautical chart with Loran A overlay pinpointed a wreck symbol about 55 miles south of Block Island, Rhode Island, and approximately 65 miles southwest of Long Island, in an area that is about 255 feet deep.

Lieutenant Commander Lee B. Findly, commanding officer of Spikefish *presents "Ten Grander's" certificates to Vice Admiral Fitzhugh Lee (center), and Rear Admiral Lloyd Mustin. Each member of the crew on board for the record setting dive was presented with a certificate.* (Photo courtesy of the Submarine Force Library and Museum.)

Admirals Mustin and Lee (on the left), and Captain Kenneth Schacht, Commander Submarine Squadron Twelve, look on as Lt. Commander Findly uses his dress sword to cut the cake commemorating his boat's 10,000th dive. (Photo courtesy of the Submarine Force Library and Museum.)

"Ten Grander's" certificate. (Photo by H. Keatts.)

A fishing charter-boat captain, who operates out of Montauk, New York, gave us Loran C numbers for the wreck site. However, he doubts that the wreck is *Spikefish*. He thinks it is the U.S. destroyer *Baldwin* (DD-624), which was sunk as a target.

The *Automated Wreck and Obstruction Information System* (AWOIS) published by the National Oceanic and Atmospheric Administration (NOAA) does not list either of the two Navy vessels, nor does it give any information in regard to the wreck symbol on the nautical chart, which is also published by NOAA.

The specifications of the two vessels are similar, the destroyer is 37 feet longer, with a 6-foot greater beam, but it displaces almost 200 fewer tons than the submarine. Because both vessels are over 300 feet long, it would be difficult to distinguish between them with a standard recording fathometer. Unless a side-scan sonar is used, divers will have to visit the site to determine if the 255-foot-deep wreck is *Spikefish* or *Baldwin*.

CHAPTER 13

World War II
U.S. Submarine Losses

This chapter, covering World War II submarine losses, is included to provide additional historic perspective. All but one of the 52 submarines were lost far from the continental United States' shores. Many are at extreme depths, beyond the range of sport divers, and at uncertain locations. Additional research may unveil new evidence to fill in gaps and alter our interpretation of available records, but one conclusion will never change. The U.S. Navy Submarine Service deterred the Japanese long enough for American industry and military buildup to reverse the early course of World War II.

The lost submarines, and the men lost with them, occupy a place of honor in the history of their country and the world, a world in which time reverses the roles of victor and vanquished. A defeated nation faces several alternatives. It may accept its lot or, if determined to achieve the objectives for which it fought, rebuild for another war. The third option is to side-step, and find another means to the same end. After World War II, Japan chose the latter course, and succeeded where she had failed militarily.

Forty-five years after V-J Day, Japan's peaceful pursuit of economic dominance, nourished by government subsidy, has penetrated the shores that once repulsed her war effort. Today, vanquished vies with victor for world-wide industrial and financial leadership. Enormous tracts of American soil, skyscrapers, hotels, resorts, golf courses, banks, and complete business enterprises have transferred to Japanese ownership. What more could a war victory have achieved for the island empire?

Japan attacked Pearl Harbor thinking that the United States, divested of her Pacific Fleet, would be unable to thwart her planned domination of the Pacific, preliminary to an invasion of North America. The immediate results were gratifying. Sunken warships and smoldering hulks remained of what had once been a formidable naval force—but the submarine base was untouched. Not one of the five submarines in for repair was damaged.

The same pattern held true in the Japanese December 10, attack on the Cavite Navy Yard in the Philippines. For some reason, their bombers initially ignored the anchored submarines of the Asiatic Fleet. Most had time to evacuate the harbor and dive to refuge on the bottom. *Sealion* (SS-*195*), was less fortunate. She was tied up at Machina Wharf, alongside the submarine *Seadragon* (SS-*194*), with the mine sweeper *Bittern* and the submarine rescue ship *Pigeon.* Unfortunately, the facility was not entirely ignored. An enemy plane delivered two strings of bombs on the area. *Seadragon* was only damaged, but aerial bombs sank *Sealion,* the first of 52 U.S. submarines that would be lost before the end of the war. If the enemy had realized what a toll submarines would exact from Japan's merchant and military fleets in the next four years, they would have been prime targets at the beginning.

While American industry was occupied in rebuilding United States naval and air strength, a thin line of undersea boats assumed the task of attacking enemy shipping, carrying supplies, ammunition, fuel and military personnel, and rescuing downed airmen. Many of the boats were obsolete and constantly under repair. Torpedoes were deficient, sparing victims that attacked in reprisal instead of sinking; or they broached and circled back to destroy the submarines that had fired them. They were attacked and sunk in error by their own forces. Inaccurate navigation charts stranded them in unfamiliar waters, and mines took a terrible toll. Still, they sank 1,314 Japanese ships totaling 5.3 million tons before the war ended.

There are 52 stories to tell, one for each of the U.S. submarines lost in bringing Japan to unconditional surrender on August 14, 1945. Based on available information that includes Japanese war records, the most likely distribution of how they were lost is:

Enemy action and or mines	– 33	Stranding	– 4
Friendly forces error	– 2	Circular torpedo run	– 2
Operational	– 3	Unknown	– 8

Enemy action and mines have been combined in tabulating the causes of loss because surfaced U.S. submarines sunk by enemy forces may have been compelled to surface by damage from a mine explosion. The lost submarines are listed in the following table in the sequence in which they were lost, with the cause of loss, where known. Those that were lost entirely due

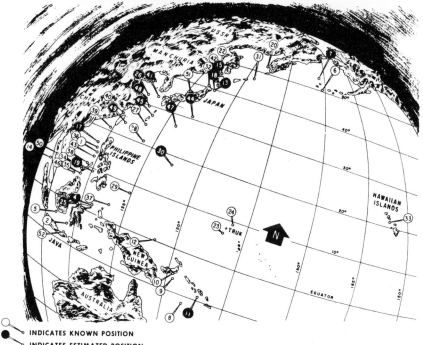

○ INDICATES KNOWN POSITION
● INDICATES ESTIMATED POSITION

POSITIONS OF SUBMARINE LOSSES

U.S. Submarine Losses—World War II
(Listed in chronological order of sinking)

Submarine	Action or Mine	Stranded	Operational	Circular Run	Friendly Forces	Still Unknown	Date of Loss
1. *Sealion*	x						12/10/41
2. *S-36*		x					1/21/42
3. *S-26**					x		1/24/42
4. *Shark*	x						2/11, 2/21/42
5. *Perch*	x						3/3/42
6. *S-27*		x					6/19/42
7. *Grunion*						x	7/30, 8/6/42
8. *S-39*		x					8/13, 8/14/42
9. *Argonaut*	x						1/10/43
10. *Amberjack*	x						2/16/43
11. *Grampus*	x						3/5, 3/6/43
12. *Triton*	x						3/15/43
13. *Pickerel*	x						4/3/43
14. *Grenadier*	x						4/22/43
15. *Runner*						x	5/28, 7/4/43
16. *R-12**			x				6/12/43
17. *Grayling*						x	9/12/43
18. *Pompano*	m						8/29, 9/27/43
19. *Cisco*	x						9/28/43
20. *S-44*	x						10/7/43
21. *Dorado**					x		10/12/43
22. *Wahoo*	x						10/11/43
23. *Corvina*	x						11/16/43
24. *Sculpin*	x						11/19/43
25. *Capelin*						x	12/9/43
26. *Scorpion*	m						1/5, 2/24/44

Cause of Loss

Submarine	Action or Mine	Stranded	Operational	Circular Run	Friendly Forces	Still Unknown	Date of Loss
27. *Grayback*	x						2/26/44
28. *Trout*						x	2/29/44
29. *Tullibee*				x			3/26, 3/27/44
30. *Gudgeon*	x						4/7, 5/11/44
31. *Herring*	x						6/1/44
33. *Golet*	x						6/14/44
34. *S-28*			x				7/4/44
35. *Robalo*	m						7/26/44
36. *Flier*	m						8/13/44
37. *Harder*	x						8/24/44
38. *Seawolf*					x		10/3/44
39. *Darter*		x					10/24/44
40. *Shark*	x						10/24/44
41. *Tang*				x			10/24/44
42. *Escolar*	m						10/17, 11/3/44
43. *Albacore*	m						11/7/44
44. *Growler*						x	11/8/44
45. *Scamp*	x m						11/9, 11/16/44
46. *Swordfish*	x						1/12/45
47. *Barbel*	x						2/4/45
48. *Kete*						x	3/20, 3/31/45
49. *Trigger*	x						3/26, 3/28/45
50. *Snook*						x	4/8, 4/20/45
51. *Lagarto*	x						5/3/45
52. *Bonefish*	x						6/18/45
53. *Bullhead*	x						8/6/45
Totals	33	2	3	4	2	8	

m = mine
*Losses not shown on chart.

to mines are identified with an "m" in the "Action or Mine" column. If a mine was considered to be a contributing factor, the column is marked "x m."

More detail on each submarine is provided in alphabetic sequence, in the pages that follow. Their exploits, awards, and the circumstances under which they were lost are described within the limits of available information. From *Albacore* to *Wahoo,* they are a chronicle of skill, dedication, and valor—a tribute to the 374 officers and 3,131 enlisted men who were left behind with 52 American submarines, after World War II had run its course.

Albacore (SS-*218*)

Albacore enjoyed a highly successful career for the two and a half years she served in World War II. From her June 1, 1942 commissioning until she sank in the heavily mined waters off Japan's islands of Honshu and Hokkaido, *Albacore* sank more combatant ships than any other submarine in the war. Her victims included the aircraft carrier *Taiho,* the light cruiser *Tenryu,* two destroyers, *Oshio* and *Sazanami,* a large patrol craft and an unidentified escort vessel. To those she added two transports, four freighters, and a medium tanker, for a total of 13 ships (74,100 tons) sunk and five ships (29,400 tons) damaged.

Enemy records indicate that a submarine was destroyed by a mine detonation in *Albacore's* patrol area on November 7, 1944. The sinking was witnessed by a Japanese patrol craft that reported seeing heavy oil, bubbles, cork, bedding, and provisions surface after the explosion.

Commander Hugh R. Rimmer and his 86-man crew share the glory of *Albacore's* exploits. The submarine was awarded the Presidential Unit Citation for four of her missions, the second, third, eighth and ninth, the patrols on which she sank enemy combatants. She also received nine battle stars for service in World War II.

Amberjack (SS-219)

Amberjack's first and last missions were in the Shortland-Rabaul-Buka area. Between mid-September and mid-October 1942, she sank two Japanese vessels, *Shirogane Maru* and *Senkai Maru.* She was then ordered to Espiritu Santo for temporary assignment to the South Pacific Air Force. Planes on Guadalcanal were so desperately in need of fuel that crashed airplanes were drained of gasoline to keep fighter planes in the air. *Amberjack* was needed for a special mission—to deliver 9,000 gallons of aviation gas, 200 hundred-pound bombs, and 15 pilots and crew members to Lunguna Roads, Guadalcanal.

On October 25, 1942 the submarine was at Laguna Point, close to her destination when her orders were changed—to unload at Tulagi, across the channel from Guadalcanal. The reason became apparent when three Japanese destroyers opened fire on American positions on the island, particularly Henderson Air Field. After dusk, *Amberjack* headed into Tulagi Harbor and unloaded her passengers and valuable, but dangerous cargo. She left for Brisbane, Australia after midnight, her mission completed.

The submarine's second patrol was west of Bougainville, with several unsuccessful attacks on enemy ships. She left on her third patrol after 12 days of refitting and relaxation, but was forced back to port for repair of minor leaks. She left Brisbane on January 26, with Lieutenant Commander John A. Bole, Jr. in command, to patrol the Solomons area. On February 3, she sank a two-masted schooner by gunfire 20 miles from Buka, while patrolling the western approaches to Buka Passage.

Amberjack was ordered to move south, through the Baka-Shortland traffic lane, to patrol east of Vella Lavella Island. While she was recharging batteries on the surface, a lookout spotted an enemy freighter estimated at 5,000 tons. Bole ordered a surface attack with five torpedoes and deck gun.

The freighter fought back with its own gun, killing Chief Pharmacy Mate Arthur C. Beeman and slightly wounding an officer. At least one torpedo struck the freighter, with resulting fire and explosions that convinced Lt. Commander Bole that the ship had been sunk. That was his report. Japanese records showed no such loss, but their war records were notoriously vague, inaccurate, or missing.

On February 13, *Amberjack* was ordered to hunt for enemy traffic throughout the entire Rabaul-Buka-Shortland area. The next day she reported recovering a downed Japanese airman from the water and taking him prisoner. She had also been forced to submerge by two enemy destroyers. That was the last message received from the submarine. On March 22, 1943 she was reported presumed lost.

Japanese war records include a report that on February 16, 1943 the torpedo boat *Hiyodori* and submarine patrol boat *No. 18* attacked a U.S. submarine in *Amberjack's* last reported location with nine depth charges following an attack by an accompanying patrol plane. Oil, bubbles, and wreckage came to the surface. It is believed that the attack sank *Amberjack,* with the loss of her 73-man crew (one had been killed in the freighter attack) and the ill-fated rescued enemy aviator. However, *Grampus* (SS-*207*) was also lost in the same area at about the same time. Either might have been the victim.

Argonaut (SS-*166*)

At the start of 1943, the United States had 80 submarines operating in the Pacific. One of the diminishing number of old V-boats still fighting the war was *V-4,* renamed *Argonaut.* She was ancient, unwieldy and slow, but she was capable of performing special missions, and had been sent to Brisbane in December 1942 for that purpose. Most others of her design had been turned over for training submarine crews by that time. She had been on defensive patrol with *Trout,* near Midway Island when the Japanese attacked Pearl Harbor, and was the first American submarine to confront the enemy at sea.

Argonaut was on the scene when the Japanese launched their attack on Midway. Her commander was Lieutenant Commander Stephen George Barchet, a former football star of the Naval Academy class of 1924. He feared that the Japanese naval force included cruisers and destroyers in numbers that would endanger his submarine. He remained submerged at 125 feet, and never attacked what turned out to be only two destroyers. That caution prompted a confrontation with his executive officer, William Schulyer Post, and eventually his own separation from the submarine service. Barchet was replaced by Lieutenant Commander John R. Pierce as commanding officer of the submarine.

Argonaut and her entire crew were lost after a severe depth charge attack that forced the submarine to the surface, where enemy destroyers circled and finished her off with deck guns. (Photo courtesy of the Submarine Force Library and Museum.)

Argonaut's moment of glory occurred on her second patrol, in support of a raid on Makin in the Gilbert Islands that was intended to divert attention and enemy forces from the American invasion of Guadalcanal. The action was conducted in August 1942 with *Nautilus* (SS-*168*), another antique, converted V-boat. On August 17, the two submarines landed Lieutenant Colonel Evans Carlson and his Second Raider Battalion of marines on the island. The small Japanese garrison was wiped out or dispersed by Carlson's Raiders, but 30 of the 222 marines in the strike force were either killed or missing. Nine who were inadvertently left behind were later captured by reoccupying enemy forces. Vice-Admiral Koso Abe had them executed as "pirates," having them beheaded, in violation of the rules of war. The admiral was later tried as a war criminal, and hanged.

Argonaut's third war patrol was conducted at a time when American submarine strength in the South Pacific was at a low ebb. Otherwise, the old V-boat would never have been ordered out on a combat mission. She arrived southeast of New Britain Island on January 10, and immediately intercepted a five-ship convoy, protected by three destroyers. A passing U.S. Army Air Corps bomber, returning from a mission, observed the action and reported that one destroyer was hit by a torpedo, but did not sink. Torpedoes also hit the two other destroyers, but they were not damaged, perhaps because of defective magnetic warheads.

A furious depth charge attack followed. One explosion blew the submarine to the surface, where she was torn apart by enemy deck guns. Then the ancient V-boat sank, taking her entire 105-man crew with her.

Barbel (SS-316)

Until the end of World War II, the U.S. Navy had no idea of why *Barbel* failed to return from her fourth war patrol. She had left Fremantle, Australia on January 5, 1945, under command of Lieutenant Commander C.L. Raguet to patrol in the South China Sea. She received instructions on January 13 to cover the western approaches to Balabac Strait and southern entrances to Palawan Passage with *Perch* (SS-*176*) and *Gabilan* (SS-*252*).

Barbel's last message was on February 3, 1945; she had been attacked with depth charges by aircraft three times that day. She promised a message with more information the next night, but was never heard from again. On February 7, she was given up as lost.

Japanese war records reveal a more complete story of *Barbel*'s disappearance. One of their planes attacked a surfaced American submarine off the southwest shore of Palowan. One of two bombs struck the submarine near the bridge, sending her under in a cloud of flame and spray. She may have been caught on the surface because of damages suffered in one of the three depth charge attacks she had undergone the day before.

The *Balao*-class submarine had sunk ten ships and damaged two, for 55,200 and 14,000 tons, respectively. She received three battle stars for her World War II service.

Bonefish (SS-223)

By 1945, the waters of Japan's main islands were heavily mined to discourage U.S. submarines from their destruction of Japanese shipping in those waters. The success of that defense became increasingly evident during 1944 as more and more American submarines disappeared without trace, and were reported as missing, and presumed lost. American submarine skippers were alerted to known concentrations of those silent sentries, while stateside research sought an effective, on-board mine-detection system.

During the last year of the war, a new frequency-modulation sonar system was installed on American submarines in the Pacific. *Bonefish* was equipped with the device; it could sense the location of a mine at a distance of about a quarter of a mile. A detected mine set off an unforgettable clanging alarm, called by submariners, "hell's bells."

Tshushima Strait between Kyushu Island and the Korean peninsula, provided Japanese shipping with access to the sea. In addition to heavy defenses, it was planted with a three-layered minefield.

On May 27, 1945, *Bonefish,* in company with *Sea Dog* (SS-*401*), *Crevalle* (SS-*291*), *Spadefish* (SS-*411*), *Tunney* (SS-*282*), *Skate* (SS-*305*), *Flying Fish* (SS-*229*), *Tinosa* (SS-*283*), and *Bowfin* (SS-*287*), left Guam to penetrate Tshushima Strait and attack enemy shipping in the Sea of Japan. All were equipped with the new F-M sonar sets, and safely transited the dangerous strait, despite a fourth layer of mines that had been installed. In 17 days, the 9 submarines sank 27 surface vessels, then safely exited with only one casualty—*Bonefish*. She had requested, and been granted permission to conduct a daylight patrol of Toyama Wan, a bay in north central Honshu. That was her last message.

Japanese records of antisubmarine attacks later explained *Bonefish's* disappearance. On June 18, 1945, a Japanese patrol boat attacked and sank an American submarine in Toyama Wan. The *Gato*-class submarine went down with her commanding officer Commander Lawrence L. Edge and his 84-man crew—from depth charges, not a mine.

Bonefish sank 31 ships (158,500 tons) and damaged 7, for 42,000 tons. She received the Navy Unit Commendation for five of her war patrols, and seven battle stars for World War II service.

Bullhead (SS-332)

Bullhead was the last American submarine sunk in World War II. She disappeared on her third mission, a patrol in the Java Sea. Like many other such losses, there was no U.S. Navy evidence to support any speculation of the cause. It took post-war examination of Japanese war records to provide the answer.

The *Balao*-class submarine, commanded by Lieutenant Commander Edward R. Holt, Jr., reported on August 6, 1945 that she had passed through Lombok Strait to take up a position off the coast of Bali. That was her last message. Other U.S. and British submarines operating in the area were unable to contact her, and she was reported missing, presumed lost.

Japanese records reflect that on August 6, 1945, the day of *Bullhead's* last report, one of their Army planes attacked a surfaced submarine in the position from which she had last reported. Ten depth charges sank the American submarine before she could escape. For ten minutes, a great amount of gushing oil and air bubbles broke the surface. It was the end of the last U.S. submarine lost in World War II.

Bullhead completed two war patrols, and was credited with four enemy ships sunk, for 1,800 tons and three damaged, totaling 1,300 tons—all by gunfire on her second mission. On her first war patrol, to the South China Sea, she bombarded Pratas Island defenses with her five-inch gun and rescued three airmen from a downed B-29 bomber after an air strike on the China coast. She was awarded two battle stars for World War II service.

Japan surrendered eight days after *Bullhead's* sinking.

Capelin (SS-289)

Capelin was one of the numerous U.S. submarines that were lost in World War II with no known cause until Japanese war records could be reviewed after the war. Like others, she departed for her last patrol and was not heard from again. She had returned from her first patrol, in the Molucca Sea, after sinking a 3,127-ton Japanese cargo ship, and may have damaged another. In the process, she was damaged by an enemy destroyer. Leaks and damages were repaired in one day, and *Capelin* departed on her final war mission on November 17, 1943, headed again for the Molucca Sea and Celebes Sea areas.

Japanese war records report that an American submarine was attacked off Kaoe Bay, Halmahera on November 23, but the attack was broken off. The U.S. submarine *Bonefish* (SS-*223*) reported a December 2 sighting of a U.S. submarine in *Capelin*'s patrol area. All that can be verified is that *Capelin*, with her commanding officer Commander Eliot E. Marshall and his 77-man crew were lost in the Celebes Sea, Molucca Passage or Molucca Sea, probably in December 1943. It was learned later that the Japanese had strewn the waters along the north coast of Celebes with mines. It is very possible that they account for *Capelin*'s disappearance.

Capelin sank two ships, for 7,400 tons of shipping. She was awarded one battle star for World War II service.

Cisco (SS-290)

It is bad enough to lose a submarine to enemy attack or a mine field. It is far worse to learn that a four-month old *Gato*-class submarine fell victim to such poor maintenance that leaking oil provided a continuous visual guide of her submerged location to enemy aircraft and surface vessels.

Cisco was commissioned May 10, 1943. She was last heard from when she left Port Darwin September 20, on her first war patrol. Lieutenant Commander James W. Coe was in command of the new submarine. Two days earlier, she had put into port for refueling, then departed to patrol in the Sulu Sea. She returned the same evening for repairs to her leaking hydraulic system, then sailed with assurance that the repairs had been made. She was never again heard from.

Japanese war records, examined after the war, include a report that a hunter-killer team of antisubmarine craft and airplanes had tracked an oil trail on the surface and carried out a successful attack on the accommodating submarine. A Japanese pilot reported that two weeks later, oil was still surfacing at the site of the sinking.

Lt. Commander Coe had completed six prior war patrols as commanding officer, three on *S-39* (SS-*144*) and three on *Skipjack* (SS-*184*). His testimony to Captain Charles A. Lockwood, Southwest Pacific Submarine Commander about Mark XIV torpedo deficiencies contributed to the ultimate realization that the Bureau of Ordnance was at fault for torpedo misses. It was the unfortunate submarine skippers, misled to place their trust in the defective weapons, who had initially borne that blame. Complaints such as Coe's overwhelmingly confirmed that the torpedoes ran too deep, and their Mark VI magnetic exploders detonated prematurely—or not at all.

Cisco never had a chance to prove her merit with either the deficient Mark XIV or its successor, the Mark XVIII electric torpedo. Leaking oil and an observant enemy sent her to the bottom on her first mission.

Corvina (SS-*226*)

Corvina left Pearl Harbor November 4, 1943 on her first war patrol, and refueled at Johnston Island two days later. It was a hazardous mission for the new *Gato*-class submarine and her commanding officer, Commander Roderick S. Rooney. The American invasion of the Gilbert Islands was impending, and *Corvina* was to patrol as close as possible to the heavily guarded island of Truk. She was there to intercept any Japanese forays against the American assault.

Early in December, three messages were transmitted to *Corvina,* requesting acknowledgment that was never received. Subsequent messages also went without response. She had disappeared. On December 23, 1943 *Corvina* was reported as missing, and presumed lost.

Japanese records report a three-torpedo attack by their submarine *I-176* on an American submarine south of Truk, on November 16, 1943. Two of the torpedoes struck the target. The time and location coincide with *Corvina*'s schedule. It appears that she was the victim. If so, she was the only American submarine to be sunk by a Japanese submarine in World War II.

Darter (SS-*227*)

The "indestructible" *Darter* earned her name after she was lost on Bombay Shoal in the difficult channels of Palewan Passage, in the Philippines. The *Gato*-class submarine, under command of Commander D.H. McClintock, played a key role in the outcome of the October 1944 Battle of Leyte Gulf on her final mission. She and *Dace* (SS-*247*) had intercepted a Japanese fleet before it could reach its objective of destroying American ships off the Leyte beachhead. The two submarines joined forces to sink Admiral Kurita's flagship, *Atago* and another cruiser *Maya.* The cruiser

Takao was damaged so severely that she remained out of action for the duration of the war.

On October 23, in pursuit of the crippled *Takao* through the tortuous turns of Palawan Passage, *Darter* grounded on Bombay shoal and ran high onto a reef. It was just after midnight, and the receding tide frustrated all efforts to free her. When it became evident that she would have to be abandoned in the hostile area, all confidential documents and equipment were destroyed, demolition charges were planted and the crew transferred over to *Dace*. The charges failed to explode. Then *Darter* began to earn her reputation as "indestructible."

Dace fired her torpedoes to destroy the stranded submarine, but they detonated harmlessly on the reef because the water was so shallow. She then fired twenty-one 4-inch shells that did damage *Darter,* but she remained intact. An enemy plane bombed her as *Dace* departed for Fremantle, but without appreciable effect. Another U.S. submarine, *Rock* (SS-*274*), tried her hand with torpedoes, but still with no effect because of the shallow waters. *Nautilus* (SS-*168*) scored 55 hits with her 6-inch gun, and reported, "It is doubtful that any equipment in *Darter* at 1131 this date would be of any value to Japan—except as scrap." When she was examined in 1962, she was still intact, appearing indestructible.

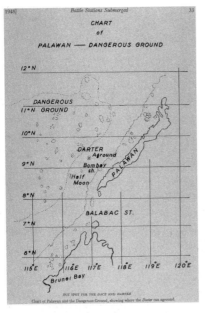

Darter aground on Bombay Shoal off southwest Palawan. Efforts to get her off the reef were unsuccessful. (Photo courtesy of the Naval Historical Center.)

Chart of Palawan showing where Darter *ran aground.* (Illustration courtesy of the Naval Historical Center.)

Darter is credited with sinking 23,700 tons of enemy shipping and damaging an additional 30,000 tons. She received the Navy Unit Commendation, with *Dace,* for her eminently successful final patrol, and four battle stars for service in World War II.

Dorado (SS-*248*)

The tragedy of war is never so poignant as when lives are lost to the weapons of one's own military. *Dorado,* a *Gato*-class submarine, was only 46 days old, en route from New London, Connecticut, to her first assignment in Panama, when she was lost in friendly waters. She was the victim of a depth charge attack by a misguided aircraft pilot who had been assigned to protect a convoy passing through the area. Standard practice imposed bombing restrictions within an area 15 miles on either side of an unescorted submarine passing through friendly waters, and 50 miles ahead and 100 miles behind her scheduled location.

The patrol plane assigned to provide air cover for the convoy reportedly received faulty instructions regarding *Dorado*'s presence in the waters. It sighted the submarine submerging on the night of October 12, 1943 and dropped three depth charges on what was taken to be a German U-boat. Several hours later the pilot attempted to exchange recognition signals with another submarine in the mistaken belief that it was *Dorado.* The submarine fired on the plane and escaped. German U-boats had been operating in the area.

A court of inquiry cited lack of evidence in its failure to reach a definite conclusion regarding *Dorado*'s loss. The indications are overwhelming that she was a victim of faulty communication that led to her destruction by military forces of her own country.

Lieutenant Commander E.C. Schneider with his new submarine and her entire crew were denied their opportunity to serve their country in World War II. They were wiped out of existence by weapons from the same arsenal they would have drawn upon to sink as much enemy shipping as possible.

Escolar (SS-*294*)

Escolar was lost on her first war mission in 1944, while leading a coordinated patrol that included submarines *Croaker* (SS-*246*) and *Perch* (SS-*176*). The "wolf pack" was designated "Millican's Marauders" for *Escolar*'s commanding officer, Commander William J. Millican. Between leaving Midway on September 23 and October 17, the three submarines maintained frequent communication. *Escolar*'s final message was that she was heading on an easterly course to a new position in the Yellow Sea.

Japanese war records carry no indication of antisubmarine activity that might account for *Escolar*'s disappearance with her 82-man crew. The waters had been strewn with mines in the general area where she might have been. On that flimsy evidence, it is assumed that she sank after detonating a mine.

Flier (SS-*250*)

Flier was lost on August 13, 1944 because she struck a mine in Balabac Strait, the Philippines, the same area where *Robalo* (SS-*273*) had disappeared three weeks earlier. The violent explosion shattered the forward starboard side of the submarine, hurling her commanding officer Lieutenant Commander John D. Crowley to the after part of the bridge and injuring several others who were sharing the bridge with him. Within seconds *Flier* went under, still driving through the water at 15 knots. Fifteen men are known to have escaped before she went down, but only eight reached the beach at Mantangula Island. They had been in the water for 15 hours.

Friendly natives guided the survivors to a coast watcher, who dispatched a message for the submarine *Redfin* (SS-*272*) to pick them up. The eight were taken aboard on the night of August 30, 1944.

Flier was awarded one battle star for her service in World War II, a single successful war patrol that had netted four freighters sunk (19,500 tons), another damaged and a tanker damaged (13,500 tons).

Golet (SS-*361*)

Golet engaged in only two war patrols. Her first resulted in no sinkings or damages to enemy ships. She left Midway on her second mission on May 28, 1944 to patrol the entire northeast coast of Honshu, Japan's main island. Heavy mining of the island's offshore waters and alert surveillance had been implemented to protect the area from the terrible toll American submarines had been exacting from Japanese marine traffic.

No communications were received from *Golet* from the time she left on patrol. Lieutenant Commander James S. Clark was in command of the new *Balao*-class submarine. He had taken over from Lieutenant Commander James M. Clement after the submarine's first mission. Eighty-two men were aboard when the submarine disappeared, with only Japanese war records to reveal how she was lost.

Enemy records revealed that a Japanese antisubmarine attack had been made on June 14 in *Golet*'s assigned patrol area. The attack brought up cork, rafts, and other debris, in addition to a large pool of heavy oil. With no other U.S. submarines in the vicinity, *Golet* was the only possible target.

Grampus (SS-*207*)

Grampus had five patrols to her credit before she left Brisbane on February 11, 1943. Her sinkings totaled six ships for a total of 45,000 tons, and two others totaling 3,000 tons were damaged. Lieutenant Commander John R. Craig was in command as she left Brisbane for patrol in the Solomon Islands area. The last communication from the submarine was received on February 12, one day out of port. It will never be known how many, if any, of the subsequent operation orders that were transmitted to *Grampus* in the next three weeks were received. On March 7, she failed to respond when she was ordered to break radio silence. She was reported lost on March 22, 1943, but where and how she was lost are still unknown.

The frequent changes of station that were radioed to the submarine over the three-week period could have located her west of Shortland, anywhere in the Shortland-Rabaul Sea area, east of Buka and Bougainville, off the west coast of Bougainville, south of Treasury Island, north of Vella Lavella, or in Vella Gulf.

Enemy war records provide a series of U.S. submarine sightings in the area. During the time period, any one or all of them might have been *Grampus*. There were two sightings on February 17, the second very close to the location of a submarine attack that damaged a 6,400-ton freighter the next day. An antisubmarine attack followed, but no results were reported.

On the afternoon of February 19, enemy seaplanes attacked a U.S. submarine, and the following day, two patrol boats found a large amount of oil on the surface in the same position. The evidence indicated that a submarine had been sunk there. Another sighting in *Grampus*'s operating area was reported on February 24, and no other U.S. submarine could have been in the reported position at that time.

If the submarine survived until March 5-6, she might have been destroyed by enemy destroyers that passed through Blackett Strait that night. The enemy ships were destroyed in subsequent action. There is no mention of any attack made by them in Japanese records—but a large oil slick was reported in the strait the next day. Perhaps that was the time and place Japanese torpedoes, depth charges, deck guns, or ramming sent *Grampus* and her 72-man crew to the bottom.

Grayback (SS-*208*)

Grayback's World War II efforts earned her eight battle stars and two Navy Unit Commendations. She ranked 20th in U.S. submarines for total tonnage sank and 24th in number of enemy ships sunk. The *Tambor*-class submarine was under command of Commander John A. Moore when she left Pearl Harbor on January 28, 1944 for the East China Sea. It was her tenth patrol.

In her first nine war missions, *Grayback* had patrolled the areas of Saipan, Guam, South China Sea, the Solomons, and the East China Sea. Her final patrol was again to the East China Sea, east of the coast of Chekiang Province, China.

Japanese records include the report of an antisubmarine attack on a surfaced submarine, on February 26, 1944. *Grayback* should have been in that position at the time of the attack. A carrier plane, "gave a direct hit at the sub, which exploded and sank immediately." Surface craft converged at the point where bubbles and an oil slick covered the water, and continued the attack. That action is almost certainly the one that ended the illustrious career of another U.S. Navy submarine in the battle for the Pacific.

Grayback was credited with an estimated 25,000 tons sunk and 25,000 tons damaged on her final patrol. Added to the totals for her first nine missions, she sank 108,900 tons and damaged almost 75,000 tons of enemy shipping.

Grayling (SS-209)

World War II had ended 22 years earlier when the nuclear powered submarine *Grayling* was launched on June 22, 1967 at the Portsmouth Naval Shipyard. Her sponsor, Miss Lori Brinker, was the daughter of Lieutenant Commander Robert M. Brinker. Brinker was in command of the *Tambor*-class submarine *Grayling* when she disappeared on her eighth war patrol in World War II. He and his crew of 75 were lost somewhere off the Philippine coast, probably during the second week of September 1943.

All but the first of *Grayling*'s war patrols produced sinkings or damage to enemy ships. Her missions between January 1942 and September 1943 are credited with five major kills totaling 20,575 tons. She patrolled the northern Gilbert Islands on her first mission, the coast of Japan on her second, and Truk on her third and fourth. She patrolled the approaches to Manila on her fifth patrol and the Tarakan area and Verde Island Passage on her sixth. Her seventh mission was the waters off northwest Borneo. Wherever she went, she inflicted damage on enemy ships.

On July 30, 1943 *Grayling* left Fremantle on her eighth war patrol, to the Philippines through Makassar Strait. She reported damaging the 6,000-ton passenger-freighter vessel *Meizan Maru* on August 19, and the next day that she had sunk a 250-ton tanker by gunfire. During her patrol she delivered supplies and equipment to guerrillas at Panay Island, first on July 31, then August 23. The latter delivery was reported by the guerrillas, the last word that was ever received regarding *Grayling*.

She was scheduled to patrol Tablas Strait until September 2, then the approaches to Manila until September 10, before returning to Pearl Harbor for refit. She was officially reported, "lost with all hands" on September 30, 1943. *Grayling* was awarded six battle stars for her World War II service. Her commanding officer was honored posthumously, when his daughter Lori was selected to sponsor the nuclear submarine *Grayling* 24 years later.

Grenadier (SS-210)

Grenadier was lost in an aerial bomb attack on April 20, 1943. She had been on patrol for several days in Lem Voalan Strait, northwest of Penang on the Malay Peninsula, then moved ten miles west in search of enemy targets. As she was preparing to attack two ships, a Japanese plane attacked, forcing her to dive. She was 120 feet down when an aerial bomb severely damaged the submarine; she came to rest on the bottom, at 270 feet. Leaks in her hull, main air induction system, and hatches were bad enough, but the stern was twisted, and a fire in the control room left her without propulsion.

Bucket brigades, pumps, and electricians worked through the next day before the submarine could be surfaced at dusk. The engines were operable, but the screw-propeller shafts were bent so badly, only one would turn—very slowly. A Japanese patrol plane attacked the crippled vessel, but was driven off by gunfire after dropping its bomb.

An enemy merchant ship accompanied by an escort vessel arrived the next morning, and took the entire crew of 76 aboard, but not before Lieutenant Commander J.A. Fitzgerald, *Grenadier*'s commanding officer, had the code machine, code books and all classified information destroyed and the submarine scuttled. The crew was imprisoned, interrogated, and tortured, but despite the brutal treatment to which they were subjected, all but four were recovered from prison camp after the war.

Grenadier could claim no sinkings on her last mission, but on her first five patrols she sank 40,700 tons of shipping and damaged 12,000 tons. Her sixth patrol was one of courage and fortitude that sustained the crew through months of torture and deprivation as prisoners of war. The submarine was awarded four battle stars for World War II service.

Growler (SS-215)

Growler's World War II career lasted slightly more than two and a half years. She was credited with sinking 17 ships, totaling 74,900 tons and damaging 7 others, for 34,100 tons. She was commissioned March 20, 1942 with Lieutenant Commander Howard W. Gilmore in command. His service was abruptly terminated on *Growler*'s fourth war patrol in the Truk-Rabaul shipping lanes.

On February 7, 1943 Gilmore attempted a surface attack on an enemy gunboat that suddenly turned in an attempt to ram the submarine. He reacted by ramming the enemy amidships at 17 knots, after a quick left full rudder. As the two vessels approached impact, the gunboat raked the bridge with machine gun fire, seriously wounding Commander Gilmore. He knew he could not get below in time, but as he lay helpless on the bridge, Gilmore ordered an emergency dive to save his command at the cost of his own life. For that selfless action, Lt. Commander Howard W. Gilmore was posthumously awarded the Medal of Honor. Only five other submariners were so honored for valor.

The remainder of *Growler's* career was with Commander Thomas B. Oakley, Jr. in command. On her eleventh war patrol, he headed a wolfpack that included *Hake* (SS-*256*) and *Hardhead* (SS-*365*). On November 8, 1944 the three submarines intercepted a convoy west of the Philippines. Oakley's order to attack was the last message ever received from *Growler*. *Hake* and *Hardhead* reported hearing a torpedo explosion and depth charges, either of which might have sunk *Growler*. One of her own torpedoes might have circled back on her, or she might have been hit by an enemy torpedo. Depth charges might have sent her to the bottom. She might even have been rammed by an enemy vessel.

Japanese war records shed no light on *Growler's* sinking. She was lost, cause unknown. Her two and a half years of war service earned her eight battle stars for service in World War II. And she will always be remembered as the submarine for which Lt. Commander Howard Gilmore sacrificed his own life.

Grunion (SS-*216*)

Grunion was lost on her first patrol, only 40 days after she arrived at Pearl Harbor on June 20, 1942. On her way there from New London, Connecticut, the new submarine had distinguished herself by rescuing 16 merchant seamen during an Atlantic storm. They were survivors of a ship that had been sunk by a German U-boat. On June 30, after ten days of training in Hawaiian waters, she left for patrol station in the Aleutians. Earlier that month the Japanese had occupied the islands of Kiska and Attu, a step closer to Alaska.

On July 10, *Grunion* was ordered to patrol north of Kiska, with Lieutenant Commander Mannert L. Abele in command. Five days later she reported that she had attacked a Japanese destroyer. Three torpedoes missed, and she was depth charged by the destroyer. Later in the day, she sank two patrol boats and damaged a third. On July 19, she was ordered, with *S-32* (SS-*137*), *Triton* (SS-*201*), and *Tuna* (SS-*203*), to be in position by July 22, patrolling the approaches to Kiska. On July 28, she reported an unsuccessful attack on unidentified enemy ships, followed by depth charges from which she escaped unscathed.

No word was received from *Grunion* after July 30, 1942 when she reported heavy antisubmarine activity at the entrance to Kiska. She had expended all but ten of her torpedoes and was ordered to proceed to Dutch Harbor. When she failed to arrive there by August 16, she was considered lost. The cause of *Grunion*'s loss with her 70-man crew has never been determined. Japanese wartime naval records, that were traditionally vague and incomplete, record no antisubmarine attack in the area at that time.

Gudgeon (SS-211)

During her three-year World War II career, *Gudgeon* earned a place of honor in the Pacific submarine fleet. She completed eleven war patrols. On those eleven missions, she was credited with sinking 25 enemy ships (166,400 tons), and damaging 8 more (over 41,900 tons). She was awarded the Presidential Unit Citation for the period of her first eight patrols, and eleven battle stars for World War II service.

Lieutenant Commander Robert A. Bonin was in command on April 7, 1944 when *Gudgeon* left on her twelfth patrol. Her area was the northern Marianas. On June 7, 1944 she was officially declared overdue, and presumed lost.

After the war, Japanese records were examined for a clue to *Gudgeon*'s disappearance. They were of no help. However, one report, dated April 18, stated that one of their planes dropped bombs on an American submarine off "Yuoh" Island. "The first bomb hit the bow, the second bomb direct on bridge. The center of the submarine burst open and oil pillars rose."

No such island as "Yuoh" exists. If the report referred to Maug Island, it would correspond with *Gudgeon*'s probable location at the time of the attack. Whatever the cause, the submarine was lost with her 78-man crew, somewhere in the northern Marianas.

Harder (SS-257)

The U.S. Navy submarine *Harder* is best known for the exploits of her commanding officer, Commander Sam D. Dealey, the "Destroyer Killer." He and the submarine lived together from her December 2, 1942 commissioning until August 24, 1944, when they died together. The war record of one is the record of the other. Commander Dealey's Congressional Medal of Honor, awarded posthumously, adds glory to the memory of the *Gato*-class submarine and her entire crew. The honor was for sinking five enemy combatant vessels on their outstanding fifth war patrol.

Harder is credited with sinking 20 1/2 enemy ships (the 1/2 was shared with *Haddo* (SS-*255*) in a joint effort), totaling 82,500 tons and damaging 7 others, for 29,000 tons. She was awarded six battle stars for World War II service.

Commander Dealey earned his nickname "Destroyer Killer" from his daring practice of allowing an attacking destroyer to bear down on his boat to one half mile, then firing a salvo of four torpedoes at the charging warship. The tactic was successful because it reduced the enemy's time to maneuver and straddled the oncoming vessel, assuring a hit, whether it veered to port or starboard to escape.

Harder's final action took place about four miles from Hermana Major Island, off the west coast of Luzon. On the morning of August 24,

Submarines Pacific Fleet

Be it known that

Commander S. D. Dealey
UNITED STATES NAVY
While Commanding Officer of the

U. S. S. Harder

has so Distinguished himself by his Conspicuous Gallantry and Extraordinary Heroism above and beyond the Call of Duty and has been awarded the

Congressional Medal of Honor

for sinking five enemy combatant vessels on his outstandingly successful fifth war patrol.

Lieutenant Commander Frank Haylor, in *Hake* (SS-*256*), saw what he identified as the old Thai destroyer *Phra Ruong* emerge from Dasol Bay in company with a minesweeper. He was terribly wrong. The minesweeper was a kaiboken, a specially equipped vessel carrying 300 depth charges and a team of highly trained antisubmarine personnel. The destroyer was the former American four-stacker destroyer *Stewart,* captured in drydock at Java, and rebuilt by the Japanese. They had renamed her *Patrol Boat No. 102.*

Hake broke off and went deep as an enemy plane bombed *Harder,* forcing her to submerge. Then the converted American destroyer moved in on *Harder* with 72 depth charges aboard, each with an effective radius of 150 feet. She dropped the charges in patterns of six, keeping contact with her target by sonar. The first set exploded at 150 feet, the next 180 feet, then 270 feet, 360 feet, and finally 450 feet. There was no safe level for *Harder.* Debris began to surface. She had sunk in 900 feet of water.

Three careers ended in the action: the submarine's, her commanding officer's and her crew's. They ended together, as they had flourished—in combat with an enemy destroyer. There could be little consolation in the fact that it had once been an American warship.

Herring (SS-233)

Herring had five war patrols in the Atlantic to her credit before she was transferred to Pacific duty in August 1943. Two of those missions produced sinkings, the 5,700-ton cargo ship *Ville du Havre,* off Casablanca on her first and the Nazi submarine *U-163* on her third.

She lost no time after reaching the Pacific. On her first patrol there, she sank the 3,948-ton *Hokazaki Maru* and the 6,072-ton *Nagoya Maru* in the East China Sea. Her seventh war mission was a disappointment, with no sinkings or damage to enemy shipping.

The *Drum*-class submarine left Pearl Harbor on May 16, 1944 on her eighth patrol, to the Kurile Islands. She stopped at Midway for refueling and left on May 21, for a May 31 rendezvous with *Barb* (SS-*220*). The two submarines had been ordered to coordinate their efforts and to agree upon patrol areas. Early in the afternoon, after the rendezvous, *Barb* was tracking two merchant vessels when she heard distant depth charging that she interpreted as an enemy attack on *Herring.*

Later in the day, *Barb* rescued a Japanese survivor from the water, and learned that *Herring* had sunk the escort for three merchantmen, two of which she had been tracking. When the escort vessel *Ishigaki* sank, the three freighters took off on their own. *Herring* sank one and the two others were later sunk by *Barb. Herring* was never again heard from. When she failed to return from patrol, she was declared missing, and presumed lost.

Japanese war records indicate June 1, 1944 as the date *Herring* was sunk, two kilometers south of Matsua Island, in the Kuriles. Her torpedoes had sunk two merchant ships, *Hiburi Maru* and *Iwaki Maru,* while they lay at anchor off the coast. A shore battery counterattack scored two direct hits on the surfaced submarine's conning tower. Bubbles covered the immediate area and heavy oil was spread over an area of about 15 square miles.

Herring's toll of enemy vessels sunk was a Nazi submarine, an Axis freighter, five Japanese freighters, and a Japanese destroyer escort warship. She was awarded five battle stars for her service in World War II.

Kete (SS-369)

Kete's loss is as much a mystery today as it was when she failed to arrive at Midway by March 31, 1945 after her second war patrol of World War II. Her first mission, in the East China Sea, had provided weather data, but little else. Her second and final patrol was to the Nansei Shoto chain of islands. She not only collected weather data for the planned invasion of Okinawa, but she maintained a rescue service for downed U.S. airmen and sank three medium freighters, for 12,000 tons.

The three freighters were sunk on the night of March 9, and the following day *Kete* reported firing four torpedoes at a cable-laying ship, with no hits. She reported having only three torpedoes left, and was ordered to leave the area on March 20 for Midway, then to Pearl Harbor for refit. Those orders were acknowledged. On March 20, *Kete* transmitted a special weather report—her last message.

Kete was awarded one battle star for her final mission in World War II.

Japanese war records show no attacks on a U.S. submarine in *Kete's* patrol area during the March 20-31, period. There were mines laid in the Nansei Shoto islands, but *Kete* was already clear of them when she made her last report.

A Japanese submarine may have torpedoed the *Balao*-class submarine, sinking her with her commanding officer Commander Edward E. Ackerman and his 86-man crew. Enemy submarines are known to have been patrolling the sea lanes *Kete* would have traveled back to Midway. One may have sunk *Kete,* and in turn been sunk by U.S. forces before having a chance to report the event to Tokyo. Three of Japan's submarines were lost in that area during the last part of March.

Kete's failure to return to Midway after her second war patrol remains a mystery in U.S. Naval records.

Lagarto (SS-371)

Lagarto, commanded by Commander Frank D. Latta, survived only seven months of World War II. She completed only one war patrol, in the

Nansei Shoto chain, supporting Admiral Halsey's Task Force 38 mission to get carrier planes to Japan undetected. *Lagarto* sank the Japanese submarine *I-371* and two small vessels on the patrol. Two others were damaged.

Her second war mission was to patrol the outer part of Siam Gulf, in the South China Sea. She teamed up with *Baya* (SS-*318*), already patrolling the area, in pursuit of an enemy convoy on May 2, 1945. The next day the two submarines exchanged contact reports and planned an attack. However, Japanese radar-equipped escort vessels kept both submarines at a distance, until, on May 4, *Baya* was forced to break off contact with the convoy. Nothing more was ever heard from *Lagarto*. She was lost with her entire complement of 86.

When Japanese war records were examined, there was no question of *Lagarto*'s fate. The radar-equipped minelayer *Hatsutaka* attacked and sank the *Balao*-class submarine in about 30 fathoms of water in the Gulf of Siam.

Lagarto was awarded one battle star for her first war patrol in World War II.

Perch (SS-*176*)

When news of the Japanese attack on Pearl Harbor reached the Philippines, the submarine *Perch* was ordered to patrol areas off Luzon and the Lingayen Gulf with *Permit* (SS-*178*), *Sailfish* (SS-*192*), and *Stingray* (SS-*186*). The Gulf was jammed with Japanese transports, but it was too shallow for submerged operation, and the submarines failed to score against the invasion force.

By February 3, 1942 *Perch* had been serviced at Port Darwin, Australia, and left on her second patrol, in the Java Sea. She was commanded by Lieutenant Commander David A. Hart. The Japanese had effectively neutralized the Philippines, and their next target was the Dutch East Indies, probably Borneo or Java. On February 25, *Perch* reported that she had made two unsuccessful attacks and had been hit by a shell that damaged her antennae. Transmission was uncertain, but she could still receive messages. Her final report, on February 27, was the sighting of two enemy cruisers and three destroyers in her patrol area. She failed to arrive in Fremantle, and was presumed lost.

After the war, Lt. Commander Hurt and all but 11 of his 64-man crew were repatriated. They were the first of the submarine force to be captured by the Japanese. The 11 who did not return had died in captivity. Hurt explained that on the night of March 1, he sighted two destroyers, and dove. He surfaced, only to be driven down again and subjected to damaging depth charges at a depth of 147 feet. Inaccurate U.S. charts of the area had misled him to believe he had at least 180 feet of water below the boat. The attack ended, and *Perch* surfaced, until two destroyers forced her to submerge again shortly before dawn, this time to 200 feet.

At dusk the crippled submarine surfaced to examine the damage. She was in such bad shape that preparations were made to scuttle her. Leaking seams and hatches, broken batteries, electrical grounds and damaged gears discouraged any attempt at repair. Nothing seemed to help. Then three enemy destroyers came on the scene, and opened fire on the defenseless hulk. Her deck gun was inoperative, and three of her torpedoes had run in their tubes from the heavy depth charge attacks. Lt. Commander Hurt ordered the boat scuttled and abandoned. Vents were opened in the engine room, and every member of the crew escaped in life belts, then waited to become prisoners of war.

Pickerel (SS-*177*)

Pickerel was never heard from after she left Midway on March 22, 1943, three days after she had left Pearl Harbor. Lieutenant Commander A.H. Alston, Jr. was in command on her seventh war mission. She was to patrol the waters off northeastern Honshu, the main island of Japan, until May 1, then return to Midway. When the submarine failed to report by May 6, she was repeatedly ordered to communicate, with no response. Air searches were unproductive, and on May 12, 1943, she and her crew of 74 were presumed lost. Others before *Pickerel* had disappeared without trace, leaving the U.S. Navy to depend on unreliable Japanese Navy records after the war for leads to when, where, and how they sank.

The target for a Japanese antisubmarine attack on April 3 off the northern tip of Honshu could have been *Pickerel,* although it was outside her patrol assignment. Another U.S. submarine, *Flying Fish* (SS-*229*) was to cover the area, but she was not due for another three days. *Pickerel* may have followed a target out of her own patrol area, or decided to check the availability of targets in someone else's territory.

Japanese naval records were not only inaccurate; they were also incomplete. An attack on the submarine may not have been reported. In some instances, Japanese vessels were sunk so soon after a confrontation that a report was never filed. Another possibility is that *Pickerel* was the victim of one of the many mines planted along the Honshu coast. The common belief is that she was sunk by an enemy depth charge attack, perhaps the one on April 3, rather than by a mine or operational accident.

Pickerel cannot be credited with sinking or damaging any enemy ships on her last patrol, but her first six missions were productive. She sank five ships, totaling 16,100 tons, and damaged ten, for 9,100 tons. She was awarded three battle stars for World War II service.

Pompano (SS-*181*)

Pompano was en route from San Francisco to Hawaii when the Japanese struck. However, the seven battle stars she was awarded for service in World War II included one for the Pearl Harbor attack. There could be no question about her entitlement to the others. She was in the thick of heavy action from her first mission on December 18, 1941 till she was lost on her seventh war patrol. Her end occurred sometime after September 25, 1943, when Japanese war records report the loss of two cargo carriers that could have been sunk only by *Pompano.* In those 21 months, she was credited with sinking ten Japanese ships (42,000 tons) and damaging four (over 55,000 tons).

Five of the *Porpoise*-class submarine's seven war patrols took her to the heavily mined waters off the coast of Japan. Her first mission was a reconnaissance patrol off Wake Island to gather intelligence for an air strike on the occupying Japanese. Her information aided the carrier raid, and she sank a 16,500-ton freighter-troop transport in the process. Her fourth war patrol took her to the Marshall Islands and the adjacent Carolines, where she damaged three tankers. The others were under the noses of the Japanese Navy, off the shores of the island chain empire.

Unfortunately for *Pompano* and U.S. submarines *Pickerel* (SS-*524*) and *Runner* (SS-*275*) before her, extremely heavy shipping losses off the islands of Honshu and Hokkaido had prompted the Japanese to saturate those offshore waters with a dense concentration of mines. It was mysterious disappearances such as *Pompano*'s that first alerted the U.S. Navy to the danger of sending submarines into the area. It is generally accepted that a mine was the cause of *Pompano*'s loss with her 76-man crew, under command of Lieutenant Commander Willis M. Thomas. She was reported overdue on October 15, 1943, presumed lost in enemy waters.

Pompano received seven battle stars for World War II service.

Robalo (SS-273)

Robalo left Fremantle June 22, 1944 on her third war patrol of World War II. On her first, west of the Philippines, she had damaged a large enemy freighter. Her second patrol was in the South China Sea, where she sank a 7,500-ton tanker. Her third mission, under Lieutenant Commander Manning M. Simmel, was back to the South China Sea, in the vicinity of the Natuna Islands.

On July 2, *Robalo* reported sighting a *Fuso*-class Japanese battleship with air cover and two destroyers as escort, just east of Borneo. That was the last communication ever received from the submarine.

Robalo was launched in May 1943. The submarine was lost 14 months later, due to an internal explosion. (Photo courtesy of the Submarine Force Library and Museum.)

A month later, at the Puerto Princessa Prison Camp on Palowan Island in the Philippines, a captured American soldier on work detail recovered a note that had been dropped from a cell window. He turned it over to the U.S. Navy, in the person of Yeoman Second Class H.D. Hough who was also a prisoner in the camp. Hough delivered the note to Trinidad Mendoza, wife of Dr. Mendoza, the local guerrilla leader. It was confirmed that *Robalo* was sunk on July 21, 1944 two miles off the western coast of Palawan Island. The cause was an explosion in her after battery compartment, probably caused by an enemy mine.

Four men swam ashore, one officer, Ensign Samuel L. Tucker, and three enlisted men, Floyd G. Laughlin, QM1c; Wallace K. Martin, SM3c; and Mason C. Poston, EM2c. They were captured and held by the Japanese, not as prisoners of war, but for guerrilla activities. They were evacuated from the island on August 15, 1944; nothing further is known of what happened to them. They may have been executed as guerillas, or the ship that carried them from Palowan Island may have been sunk before reaching its destination.

Robalo was stricken from the Navy list on September 16, 1944. She was awarded two battle stars for World War II service.

Runner (SS-275)

The *Gato*-class submarine *Runner* was laid down at the Portsmouth Navy Yard the day after the Japanese launched their attack on Pearl Harbor. Nineteen months later she was presumed lost, on her third war patrol. The submarine had torpedoed five Japanese cargo ships on her first patrol, but none was confirmed as being sunk. She barely survived a near miss from an enemy patrol bomber that crippled her sound gear and the power supply for both periscope hoists.

Her second patrol was to lay a minefield off Pedro Blanco Rock. Then she headed for Hainan Straits, off the mainland of China, where she attacked a freighter. The sound of a ship breaking up was heard over her sound gear, but a sinking could not be confirmed.

Runner left Midway on May 27, 1943 for her third war patrol, to the Kurile Islands and the northern approaches to Japan. The Japanese had concentrated on mining the waters off Honshu, mines that probably sank *Runner.* She was never heard from again, but captured Japanese records indicate that she sank the cargo ship *Seinan Maru* on June 11, in Tsgaru Strait, off Hokaido, and the passenger-cargo vessel *Shinryu Maru* on June 26, off the Kurile Islands. She was reported presumed lost by the Navy in July, and was awarded one battle star for World War II service.

R-12 (SS-89)

R-12 was 24 years old when she was lost on June 12, 1943, a World War II casualty of operational failure, not enemy action. She was commissioned

R-12 *was one of eight U.S. submarines lost from unknown cause during World War II.* (Photo courtesy of the Submarine Force Library and Museum.)

September 23, 1919, and was decommissioned December 7, 1932—nine years before the bombing of Pearl Harbor. She remained in the Reserve Fleet for seven and one-half years, until war threatened. Then she was reactivated on July 1, 1940. By May 1943, she was training submariners at Key West.

During a torpedo practice approach on June 12, *R-12* prepared to dive, with two Brazilian naval officers aboard as observers. Lieutenant Commander Edward E. Shelby shared the bridge with another officer and three enlisted men. As the preparations to dive were completed, the collision alarm sounded from below. The forward battery compartment was flooding. Although orders were given immediately to blow the main ballast and secure all hatches, the submarine plummeted to the bottom in 600 feet of water. She was underwater in an estimated 15 seconds after the alarm sounded.

Forty two officers and men were lost, including the two Brazilian observers. The loss of life would have been greater, but 16 enlisted men were not aboard because they were on liberty at the time of the mishap. A court of inquiry determined that the probable cause was a faulty torpedo tube.

Scamp (SS-277)

Scamp was lost in November 1944 on her eighth war patrol. The exact date, location, and cause can only be assumed from post-war analysis of Japanese war records. The submarine was last heard from on November 9, while on patrol in the Bonin Islands. The *Gato*-class submarine, under command of Commander J.C. Hollingsworth, was ordered from there to the coast of Japan's main island, Honshu. She was directed to take up lifeguard duty there in support of B-29 bombing attacks on Tokyo. Japanese mines had been laid in those waters to deter American submarines from sinking Japanese shipping. That was the extent of U.S. Navy information to account for the fact that *Scamp* was never heard from again.

Enemy war records include reference to a November 11, 1944 Japanese patrol plane attack on what appeared to be oil trails left by a submarine. A coast defense vessel was directed to the scene, and made three runs, dropping 70 depth charges into the waters under the slick. A large pool of oil was the only evidence that the target had been hit. The same day, another U.S. submarine, *Greenling* (SS-213), received a garbled message that might have been from *Scamp*, but nothing was sighted.

According to Japanese records, five days later two antisubmarine attacks were made in the area, "resulting in great explosive sounds." They may have signaled the end of *Scamp*. It is possible that she was first damaged by a mine, accounting for the oil trail, survived the first depth charge attack, and lasted for five more days until she was finally destroyed.

Scamp's seven patrols accounted for six ships sunk (49,000 tons) and eight damaged (40,000 tons). She was awarded seven battle stars for World War II service.

Scorpion (SS-278)

Scorpion was lost somewhere in the northern East China or Yellow Sea on her fourth war patrol. She left Midway on January 3, 1944, under command of Commander M.G. Schmidt, after three prior missions. The first took her to the approaches to Tokyo, where she planted mines and sank two freighters, two patrol boats, and four sampans, while badly damaging a 100-ton patrol craft.

Her second patrol was to the Yellow Sea. There, she sank the 10,000-ton freighter *Azan Maru* and the passenger-cargo ship *Kokuryu Maru.* On her third mission, to the Marianas, she damaged a Japanese oiler. After three missions, she had accounted for more than 24,000 tons of enemy vessels sunk and 16,000 tons damaged.

Two days after leaving Midway on her fourth patrol, *Scorpion* contacted *Herring* (SS-*233*), a nearby submarine that was returning from patrol. She attempted to transfer an injured seaman to the other vessel, for his return to Midway for treatment, but the effort was thwarted by heavy seas. If the transfer had succeeded, one American seaman would have survived the loss of *Scorpion,* with her 76-man crew.

Japanese war records were reviewed for evidence of the cause of *Scorpion*'s disappearance, but there were no antisubmarine attacks that could be linked in time and location to her schedule. However, the entrance to the Yellow Sea had been laid with Japanese mines, a fact that was not realized by the U.S. Navy until after *Scorpion* was reported missing on March 6, 1944, and presumed lost. The mines were the most probable cause of her sinking.

Scorpion's first war mission had been to lay American mines in Japanese waters. Her last was to fall victim to Japanese mines laid by the enemy in its own waters.

Sculpin (SS-191)

Sculpin's service to the Navy began during her shakedown cruise, on May 23, 1939. The *Gato*-class submarine helped to locate her sunken sister ship *Squalus* (SS-*192*), then established communication with the trapped crew and assisted in their rescue and salvage of the vessel. Their paths would cross again during World War II.

The submarine completed nine war patrols in the Pacific. She scored sinkings or damage to enemy ships on all but her third and ninth missions. Like all other submarines in the war, the persistent complaint of her

Members of Sculpin's *crew with the submarine's battle flag showing destroyed enemy vessels. The small flags with the rising sun represent Japanese warships.* (Photo courtesy of the Submarine Force Library and Museum.)

commanding officer and crew was the deficiency of the Mark XIV torpedoes and their equally defective magnetic exploders. Potential victims became the hunters, and missed opportunities set the stage for reprisal by enemy antisubmarine attacks.

Her first eight patrols took *Sculpin* to the coast of the Philippines, east of Celebes, Molukka Sea, South China Sea, the Solomons, the Aleutians, and the East China Sea. Her ninth mission was to intercept enemy forces attempting to leave Truk to oppose the forthcoming U.S. invasion of Tarawa, in the Gilbert Islands. She left Pearl Harbor on November 5, 1943 then refueled at Johnston Island, leaving there November 7, with Commander Fred Connaway in command. Commander John P. Cromwell was also aboard. During the patrol, he was promoted to captain and designated to command a three-submarine attack group, including *Sculpin*.

No messages were received from *Sculpin* after she left Johnston Island. The surviving members of her crew explained what had happened to her after their repatriation from a Japanese prisoner of war camp when the war ended. The submarine had arrived on station November 16, and made contact with a large, high-speed convoy two nights later. *Sculpin* was attacked and damaged. When she attempted to come up to periscope depth, her depth gauge failed, damaged by the attack. Without depth readings, the submarine popped through the surface like a cork. She was an easy mark for enemy destroyer deck guns, and had to be abandoned.

Captain Cromwell possessed vital information regarding the planned assault of the Gilbert Islands. Rather than take the risk of Japanese interrogation that might pry the secrets from him, he remained aboard the submarine when she went down. For that, he was posthumously awarded the Medal of Honor.

Forty-two of the crew were picked up by the destroyer *Yamagumo.* One badly injured sailor was thrown overboard, and the others were taken to Truk for intensive questioning. All 41 were placed on two aircraft carriers returning to Japan, with 20 Americans on one and 21 on the other.

On December 2, 1943 the Japanese aircraft carrier *Chuyo,* carrying 21 *Sculpin* survivors, was sunk by the U.S. submarine *Sailfish* (SS-*192*). Twenty Americans had perished at the hands of an American submarine; one clambered up the side of a passing enemy destroyer, and was saved.

Sailfish, the submarine that sank the Japanese aircraft carrier had been renamed. She was originally *Squalus,* the submarine *Sculpin* had saved four and a half years earlier.

Sculpin sank nine enemy ships for 42,000 tons and damaged ten, totaling 63,000 tons. She was awarded eight battle stars, in addition to the Philippine Presidential Unit Citation.

Sealion (SS-*195*)

The distinction of being the first U.S. submarine lost in World War II fell to *Sealion.* It was an unwelcome recognition that her crew would gladly have traded for even one mission against the enemy. When the war started (December 8, in the Philippines), she was being overhauled at the Cavite Navy Yard, within four days of scheduled completion. Two days later, most of the boats had been ordered out on patrol, but *Sealion* was still two days short of operational status. She and the submarine *Seadragon* (SS-*194*) were still tied up shortly after noon on December 10, when two waves of Japanese planes struck the submarine base.

The first bombs fell several hundred yards astern of *Sealion.* Her only possible defense against the air attack was machine gun fire, futile against the high altitude of the attacking enemy planes. Lieutenant Commander R.G. Voge, in command, ordered all hands below for better protection. On the second run, two bombs struck with disastrous effect. The first exploded alongside the conning tower, wounding three men in the control room. A fragment of the same bomb drove through the conning tower of *Sealion's* neighbor, *Seadragon,* and killed Ensign Sam Hunter.

The second bomb followed almost immediately; it exploded in *Sealion's* engine room, killing four of the crew and flooding the compartment. As the submarine settled by the stern, the torpedo room also flooded, sending

Sealion to the shallow bottom, listing to starboard, with almost half of her main deck below water.

Survivors scrambled aboard *Seadragon,* also damaged, but still afloat and destined to survive the war with a brilliant war record. She was towed into the channel by the rescue ship *Pigeon,* which had also been tied up for repair of a damaged rudder. Local repair facilities were demolished in the air raid, and the closest maintenance facility was 5,000 miles away. There was no hope of salvaging *Sealion.* She was stripped of her valuable navigational, communication, and detection equipment, then scuttled on Christmas Day, the first U.S. Navy submarine victim of World War II enemy action.

Seawolf (SS-*197*)

The enemy failed to stop *Seawolf* in 14 war missions that netted her 27 enemy ships sunk (108,600 tons) and 13 damaged (69,600 tons). Her patrols had taken her from northern Luzon when the war began, to the China coast, East China Sea, South China Sea, Indonesia, and the Caroline Islands. In addition to her bounty of enemy shipping, the *Sargo*-class submarine delivered ammunition to besieged defenders of Corregidor, and performed photographic reconnaissance of Peleliu Island, in the Palaus, for an American assault. She picked up a Captain Young from Tawitawi, Sulu Archepelago on a special mission.

Seawolf's record was remarkable, but she was not indestructible; she was sunk on her 15th war patrol after delivering stores and army personnel to Samar, between the Philippines and New Guinea. She refueled at Manus on September 29, 1944 and left for Samar the same day. She and *Narwhal* (SS-*167*) exchanged radar recognition signals in the Moratai area on October 3, *Seawolf*'s last communication.

Shortly after the exchange of signals with *Narwhal,* the American destroyer escort *Shelton* was torpedoed and sunk by a Japanese submarine. Another destroyer escort, *Rowell,* and two carrier planes from *Midway*

During 15 war patrols, Seawolf *sank 27 enemy ships, and damaged 13. Total tonnage for ships sunk and damaged were 108,600 and 69,600.* (Photo courtesy of the Submarine Force Library and Museum.)

Photos taken through Seawolf's *periscope. The Japanese destroyer was hit by one torpedo, breaking the ship in two.* (Photo courtesy of the Submarine Force Library and Museum.)

converged on the area to search for the enemy. One of the planes sighted a submerging submarine, and dropped two bombs on it. The site was dye-marked, and *Rowell* attacked with "hedgehogs," circular patterns of 24 contact charges fired simultaneously ahead of an attacking ship to detonate against the hull of a submerged submarine. *Rowell's* second pass was followed by underwater explosions that brought debris to the surface.

Seawolf was never heard from again. She was announced overdue from patrol, and presumed lost on December 28. American naval power had accomplished what the Japanese Imperial Navy could not do. It sank *Seawolf,* with her commanding officer, Lieutenant Commander Albert M. Bontier and his 81-man crew. Seventeen Army passengers were also aboard when the submarine was lost. Japanese war records credit their submarine *RO-41* with sinking *Shelton* on October 3, then returning safely to Japan.

Seawolf was awarded 13 battle stars for her outstanding role in World War II.

Shark (SS-174)

When it became evident that the defense of Corregidor Island could only be a holding action, the Dutch East Indies assumed increasing strategic importance to the American cause. Admiral Thomas C. Hart transferred his Asiatic Fleet headquarters to Surabaya, Java. After Japanese bombs destroyed all the American flying boats, he left the Philippines by submarine, in *Shark*. That was the submarine's first war patrol.

She left on her second mission on January 5, 1942 commanded by Lieutenant Commander L. Shane, Jr. Her patrol took her to the harbor entrance on the island of Ambon (Amboina) to protect against a possible enemy attack. Heavy enemy air raids on January 25, seemed to confirm that expectation. *Shark* joined a submarine group to reconnoiter a large enemy move south through Molukka passage, between Celebes and New Guinea. Her station was changed several times in response to reported enemy movements threatening Ambon.

On February 2, *Shark* reported to Surabaya that she had missed on a torpedo attack, and had been depth charged ten miles off Tifore Island. Five days later her commander was criticized for reporting an empty enemy cargo ship heading northeast. Such transmissions provided headquarters with little significant information. However, they could serve the enemy by identifying an area to be avoided because it was under U.S. surveillance.

On February 8, the submarine was ordered to proceed along the north coast of Celebes to Makassar Strait, between Celebes and Borneo. She was ordered to report information, but nothing more was heard from *Shark*. On March 7, she was presumed lost. Several Japanese reports of antisubmarine action have been considered in trying to determine what happened to her. The most likely possibility is a February 11, 1942 attack on a submarine east of Menado on northern Celebes.

Shark (SS-314)

SS-*314* is referred to as *Shark II* by some sources, but she was not the second U.S. Navy vessel to bear the name Shark; she was the sixth. Her immediate predecessor, *Shark* (SS-*174*), was lost in February 1942. *Shark* (SS-*314*) followed on October 3, 1944 after sinking a Japanese ship that was carrying 1,800 American prisoners of war from Manila to Japan. That was a sinking her crew would rather not have claimed.

Post-war review of Japanese war records revealed the sinking and ensuing antisubmarine depth charging of the American submarine. Bubbles, heavy oil, clothes, cork, and other debris surfaced after the attack.

Commander Edward N. Blakely was in command of the *Balao*-class submarine and her 86-man crew when she was lost. On two prior patrols, to the Mariana Islands, then to the Volcano and Bonin Islands, she sank five enemy ships, for 32,200 tons and damaged two, that totaled 9,900 tons.

Shark was awarded one battle star for World War II service.

Snook (SS-279)

Commander John F. Walling was in command when the *Gato*-class submarine *Snook* left Guam March 25, 1945. She was part of a three-submarine patrol group, including *Burrfish* (SS-*312*) and *Bang* (SS-*385*), that was to patrol Luzon Strait, the south coast of China, and the east coast of Hainan. It was also to perform lifeguard duty for downed airmen, if so directed. *Snook* was forced to return to Guam for one day of repairs, then she followed the others to their first assignment.

Snook transmitted weather reports until April 1, when she was ordered to join an attack group under Commander Cassidy in *Tigrone* (SS-*419*). Cassidy maintained contact with *Snook* until April 8, then heard no more from her. She was lost, but the Navy had no idea how or when.

After the war, Japanese war records were examined for some inkling of why *Snook* disappeared with neither warning nor trace. There was nothing, no mines she might have stumbled into nor antisubmarine attacks to explain her loss. There were Japanese submarines in the area, however. One might have torpedoed *Snook,* then become one of the five Japanese submarines that were sunk in the area in April and May, perhaps with no chance to report the sinking of the American submarine and her 84-man crew.

Snook sank 22 enemy ships (123,600 tons) and damaged 10 (63,200 tons). She earned seven battle stars for her World War II service.

Swordfish (SS-193)

The *Sargo*-class submarine *Swordfish* was reported missing, and presumed lost on her 13th war patrol, the victim of unknown causes. She was last heard from on January 3, 1945 when her commanding officer Commander Keats E. Montrose acknowledged orders to stay clear of the Nansei Shoto area of Okinawa while carrier-based air strikes were under way. On January 12, the U.S. submarine *Kete* (SS-*369*) contacted an unidentified submarine by radar while patrolling off the Okinawa coast. Four hours later, heavy depth charging of the area was heard. It is believed that the attack may have been directed against *Swordfish.*

There are no references to the depth charging in Japanese war records, but they were frequently incomplete and inaccurate. It is known, however, that

The officers and crew of Swordfish, *in early February 1944, at the end of their tenth war patrol, off Tokyo.* (Photo courtesy of the Submarine Force Library and Museum.)

the coast of Okinawa was heavily laid with mines in defense against an expected American assault. Either possibility may account for *Swordfish* disappearing.

On her first 12 missions, *Swordfish* sank 21 ships, for 113,100 tons and damaged 8, totaling 45,800 tons. She was awarded the Navy Unit Commendation for her first, second and fourth war patrols, and eight battle stars for World War II service.

S-26 (SS-131)

World War II was only seven weeks old when Lieutenant Commander E.C. Hawk lost *S-26* on her second war patrol; she had made no enemy contact on her first, and was not about to have any. The S-boat was headed from Balboa, Canal Zone to her patrol station on January 24, 1942 accompanied by three sister boats, *S-21* (SS-*126*), *S-29* (SS-*134*), and *S-44* (SS-*155*), and the escort vessel *PC-460*. At 10:10 p.m. the group was about 14 miles west of San Jose Light in the Gulf of Panama, when the escort vessel visually signaled that she was leaving, and the submarines were to proceed on their own. The message was never received by *S-26;* she proceeded on course until *PC-460* plowed into the starboard side of her torpedo room without warning.

Lt. Commander Hawk was sharing the bridge with his executive officer, Lieutenant Robert E.M. Ward and two enlisted men at the time of the collision. The rest of the crew were trapped below deck when the submarine sank rapidly in 300 feet of water. One of the enlisted men on the bridge was also lost, for a total of 48 casualties. Only three of the crew survived, the two officers and one enlisted man who had been on the bridge.

S-26 was lost in a collision with a U.S. escort vessel in the Gulf of Panama, about 14 miles west of San Jose Light. She sank in 300 feet of water. (Photo courtesy of the Submarine Force Library and Museum.)

Salvage efforts were launched immediately, but attempts to raise the submarine from her 300-foot grave were unsuccessful. Twenty months later, on October 7, 1943, *SS-44*, one of the S-boats in the formation when *S-26* was sunk, was also lost, but that was after she had been credited with sinking three ships and damaging a fourth in four war patrols. *S-26* was denied that opportunity.

S-27 (SS-*132*)

S-27 had only one war patrol, a reconnaissance mission in June 1942 that ended her career without enemy action. Lieutenant H.L. Jukes took the submarine into the northern perimeter of the war with Japan, to scout the area around Constantine Harbor on Amchitka Island, in the Aleutians. The U.S. Navy was interested in Amchitka, and the enemy had occupied Kiska Island, only 60 miles to the west. By June 19, the reconnaissance was completed, and *S-27* headed out of the area.

The days are long in the Aleutians during the summer months, and days are periods of submergence for submarines in a war zone. When *S-27* surfaced at 10 p.m. on June 19, her batteries were low. She was not equipped with radar or fathometer, and navigation was by dead reckoning. Jukes selected a position well off shore for the lengthy recharging process. A heavy fog obscured the drift of about 5 miles from her position that was caused by the currents. Again relying on dead reckoning, Jukes ordered the submarine ahead on one engine while using the other for charging.

Almost at once, the submarine struck hard onto a reef about 400 yards offshore of Amchitka Island. The torpedo room and the battery room both flooded. Chlorine gas was being generated by the mixture of seawater and

S-27 *struck a reef about 400 yards from Amchitka Island (Aleutians) and rolled into a rocky basin. The submarine was abandoned.* (Photo courtesy of the Submarine Force Library and Museum.)

battery acid. *S-27* was tipped to an 8°-12° angle, and the situation was desperate. Six dispatches were transmitted, but only one was picked up, and that failed to include her position.

The boat was abandoned, and the entire crew made it safely to shore in a well disciplined operation. Food, arms and ammunition were salvaged from the submarine and assembled on the beach. The following day, the crew set out for the village on the other side of the island. They found it deserted and demolished, except for a church and two other buildings. Lieutenant Jukes set up a military camp that served until a PBY sighted them five days later. It, and three other PBY's that flew in the next morning, safely evacuated the entire crew.

S-28 (SS-133)

To this day no one knows why *S-28* was lost, but it was not because of enemy action. The old S-boat had been performing training exercises off Oahu with the Coast Guard cutter *Reliance* on July 4, 1944 when she disappeared without warning. The two vessels were only about four miles apart when *S-28* submerged. *Reliance* maintained sound contact with her for about an hour, then lost all signs of the submerged submarine. There were no explosions or other unusual signs, nor distress signals to account for the disappearance of the 20-year-old S-boat—only a diesel oil slick over her position.

Lieutenant Commander Jack G. Campbell was in command of her 40-man crew when *S-28* was lost. There were also ten trainees aboard the submarine at the time. The mission was Campbell's first submarine command—and it lasted only two short weeks.

The court of inquiry that investigated the sinking determined that, "It resulted from either a material casualty or an operating error of personnel, or both, and that depth control was never regained. The exact cause of the loss of *S-28* cannot be determined." It cleared the officers and crew of any negligence or inefficiency. Salvage of the vessel was out of the question, because of the 1,400-fathom depth in the area of the sinking.

S-28 had completed seven war patrols before her assignment to training exercises because of her obsolete design and frequent mechanical failures. On her last patrol, she sank the 1,368-ton converted gunboat *Katsura Maru No. 2* in the northern Kuriles. She was awarded one battle star for World War II service.

S-36 (SS-*141*)

Submarine commanders operating in the far reaches of the Pacific had to cope with a variety of problems over which they had no control. Not only were their highly touted magnetic-influence torpedoes defective, but U.S. charts of treacherous waterways were inaccurate. Lieutenant Commander John R. McKnight Jr., commanding *S-36,* was a victim of that deficiency. Early in the pre-dawn hours of January 20, 1942 he was headed for Surabaya, Java through the dangerous waters of Makassar Strait, between Celebes and Borneo.

McKnight knew nothing about the currents, channels, or obstacles that confronted him. He was navigating by dead reckoning in foul weather when *S-36* ran aground on Taka Bakang reef at the southern end of the strait. Her hull was pierced by the coral, flooding her forward battery room. The threat of seawater and battery acid generating deadly chlorine gas was enough of a problem, but there seemed to be no way to get the boat off the reef without help, help that was not available. McKnight assessed the situation and decided to send out an uncoded message that his command was aground and in danger of sinking.

The submarine *Sargo* (SS-*188*) intercepted the call and relayed it to headquarters in Surabaya. A Dutch launch from Makassar City, Celebes, took off about half the crew the next morning. The others remained on board with McKnight, who had decided that he would try to save the submarine. As weather conditions worsened, the effort seemed more and more futile. Meanwhile, the uncoded message might bring a Japanese warship to the site. When the Dutch steamer *Siberoet* arrived on January 21, McKnight scuttled *S-36.* He and the balance of the crew arrived at Surabaya aboard the Dutch vessel. They were the victims of inadequate navigational charts of unfamiliar, dangerous waters.

S-39 (SS-*144*)

Before the 17-year-old *S-39* was lost, she had sortied on four earlier war missions that cost the enemy a 5,000-ton freighter on her first patrol and a 5,000-ton tanker on her third. She had sought the enemy in and around the Philippines, the South China Sea, and the Solomon Islands. The start of her fifth mission was marked with a series of delays that seemed to portend disaster. Twice, she had been forced back to Brisbane by mechanical problems. Then, on her third try, her executive officer was stricken by pneumonia, and was put ashore on August 10, 1942 at Townsville Harbor.

The submarine, under command of Lieutenant Francis E. Brown, was due to be east of Rossel Island, off the southeast tip of New Guinea, three days later. On August 14, already one day late due to heavy southeast winds, *S-39* arrived at her destination. She struck a reef south of Rossel Island with such force that her bow came out of the water and she toppled over to port, with the sea breaking over her stern.

The problem worsened despite backing the engines, blowing the ballast tanks, and emptying the fuel tanks to lighten the boat. That only helped the heavy surf carry the lightened craft higher onto the reef. To keep her steady and as low on the reef as possible, the empty fuel and ballast tanks were flooded. In the morning, when the tide rose, Brown managed to back *S-39* off about 50 feet, but the action forced water into her ruptured tanks, she heeled to port, and struck bottom again.

Brown recognized that there was no hope of saving his boat. He sent word to Brisbane, and the Australian Navy responded that the tug *Katoomba,* would arrive the next morning. *S-39* had settled to a 60° list and live torpedoes were being jostled by the incessant pounding of the surf. As a safety measure, all of the submarine's torpedo warheads were disconnected and those in the tubes were fired.

By the time the Australian rescue tug arrived, 32 men had transferred from *S-39* to a nearby reef as a precaution against the crippled submarine capsizing; 12 others remained aboard until *Katoomba* arrived at noon. By mid-morning on August 16, the entire crew was aboard, and *S-36* was left to be demolished by the sea and reef. There would be little left if the enemy should chance on the site, and there was little new technology in the aged S-boat to benefit the Japanese. The crew arrived safely at Townsville, Australia, on August 19, and were reassigned. Lieutenant Brown, by then Lieutenant Commander Brown, was later lost when his command *S-44* was sunk on October 7, 1943, by a Japanese destroyer.

S-39 was seen from the air in 1974.

S-44 (SS-*155*)

It takes only one mistake to transform a successful wartime career into an absolute disaster. After four successful war patrols, *S-44* surfaced to sink a small merchant ship with her deck gun—and found herself looking into the guns of an enemy destroyer. She got off one shot, and was blasted by a responding salvo. The damage prevented her from submerging—until her compartments filled with water from hits on the control room, the conning tower, and her forward battery room. A pillow case was raised in surrender, but the shelling continued as the submarine sank.

Eight men are believed to have escaped, but only two survived, Chief Torpedoman's Mate Ernest A. Duva and Radioman Third Class William F. Whitmore. They were picked up by the destroyer, taken to Paramishuro for interrogation, then to the Naval Interrogation Camp at Ofuna before spending a year in the Ashio copper mines as prisoners of war.

Lieutenant Commander Francis E. Brown, *S-44*'s commanding officer had survived the sinking of his prior command, *S-39*, when she foundered on a reef off the southeast coast of New Ireland in August 1942. His entire crew survived that disaster.

S-44's final war mission was to patrol the northern Kuriles, a departure from the locale of her first four patrols, all in the Solomon Islands area. She had claimed a victim on each of them, a small freighter on the first, a converted gunboat *Keijo Maru* on the second, and the heavy cruiser *Kako* on her third. The big warship was sunk with a salvo of four torpedoes near Kavieng, off New Ireland, while returning from a Japanese victory in the First Battle of Savo Island. Three United States and one Australian heavy cruiser had been sunk in that naval battle, one of the worst Allied surface ship defeats of the war. *S-44*'s success was a face-saver for the U.S. Navy, a morale booster for every submariner and an ego stimulant for the entire *S-44* crew. It was almost an anti-climax when she only damaged an enemy destroyer on her fourth patrol.

Nearly all the old S-boats had been withdrawn from combatant roles for training assignments when *S-44* was lost. She was the last of her class to be sunk in enemy action. *S-28* was later sunk, on July 4, 1944 but in a training exercise off Hawaii, not an enemy confrontation.

Tang (SS-*306*)

Tang survived for only one year after her commissioning on October 15, 1943. It was a memorable year for the *Balao*-class submarine, her commanding officer, Commander Richard H. O'Kane, and the 86 men of her crew. She sortied on five war missions, patrolling the waters of Truk,

Crewmen from Tang *helping Navy fliers aboard. The submarine rescued 22 downed airmen during a two-day carrier based air strike at Truk.* (Photo courtesy of the Submarine Force Library and Museum.)

Saipan, Palau, Davao, East China Sea, Yellow Sea, and the southern coast of Honshu.

In her five patrols, *Tang* sank 31 ships for a total of 227,800 tons and damaged an additional 4,100 tons. With all that to her credit, she still found time to rescue 22 Navy airmen during carrier-based strikes at Truk on April 30 and May 1, 1944. *Tang* was awarded the Presidential Unit Citation twice. She received four battle stars for World War II service, and her commanding officer received the Congressional Medal of Honor. Commander O'Kane had served as executive officer of the very successful *Wahoo* before taking command of *Tang.*

On September 27, 1944 *Tang* left Midway for Formosa Strait on her fifth war patrol. Between October 10 and October 24, she sank 13 enemy ships with 22 of her 24 torpedoes. The last two were fired at a transport that had been damaged, but needed another hit before she would go under. Torpedo number 23 ran true, but the 24th curved sharply and circled back on *Tang.* Emergency maneuvers averted a broadside hit by the errant missile, but it struck the stern of the submarine with a violent detonation that caused broken limbs among the crew as far forward as the control room. Three compartments flooded, and the ship went down by the stern.

Tang settled on the bottom at 180 feet, but 13 crewmen managed to escape from the forward compartment to join 9 officers and men who had been on the bridge. Only 9 of the 22, including Commander O'Kane and two other officers, survived eight hours in the water until they were picked up by a Japanese destroyer escort. After interrogation, they spent the rest of the war in Japanese prison camps.

Destruction by one's own torpedo at the end of one of the war's most successful missions, was a somber, thought-provoking end to *Tang's* glorious one-year career. If torpedo number 24 had been fired first instead of last, 13 Japanese vessels may have been spared at the expense of *Tang's* impressive war record. Or, with only the first 23 torpedoes aboard, *Tang* might have survived to continue her attacks on Japanese shipping until the war's end.

Trigger (SS-237)

For more than three years, *Trigger* had an illustrious World War II career. She was awarded the Presidential Unit Citation for 3 of her 12 war patrols. Her missions took her to the Aleutians, the Japanese home islands, New Guinea, East China Sea, the Carolines, Palau and to the northern Nansei Shoto area, where her career finally came to an end. She is credited with sinking 27 enemy ships (180,600 tons) and damaging 13 (102,900 tons).

When *Trigger* left Guam March 11, 1945 on her twelfth war patrol, she was to provide rescue service for carrier-based aircraft, while conducting a normal offensive patrol in the northern area of Nansei Shoto. She reported sinking a freighter and damaging another from a convoy that continued west into an area labeled in captured enemy documents as "restricted." The Navy assumed that meant it had been mined. *Trigger* was ordered to track the convoy through the area, and chart a safe passage through the mine field. However, the submarine had been held down by the convoy's escort vessels for so long, she lost contact with the convoy.

On March 26, *Trigger* was directed to join *Sea Dog* (SS-401) and *Threadfin,* (SS-410) in a wolf pack named "Earl's Eliminators." The order required acknowlegment, which was never received. However, she did send a weather report on the same day—her last message. When she failed to return to Midway by May 1, 1945, she was reported as presumed lost on her twelfth mission.

Japanese war records provide a likely explanation of *Trigger's* loss. The Japanese repair ship *Odate* was sunk on March 27, precipitating a two-hour antisubmarine attack by planes and surface ships on the American submarine. The reprisal attack was heard by nearby U.S. submarines *Silversides* (SS-236), *Sea Dog, Hackleback* (SS-295), and *Threadfin.* *Threadfin* reported, "many distant strings of depth charges and several

A Japanese destroyer photographed through the periscope of Trigger. *A hit just forward of the bridge separated the bow from the enemy warship.* (Photo courtesy of the Submarine Force Library and Museum.)

heavy explosions . . . It sounded as though someone was getting quite a drubbing." No other submarine in the area reported being the target of such an attack. It could only have been *Trigger.*

Her illustrious career earned *Trigger* eleven battle stars for World War II service, and the Presidential Unit Citation for her fifth, sixth and seventh war patrols.

Triton (SS-201)

Triton was awarded five battle stars for her role in World War II. She was credited with sinking 16 ships, totaling almost 65,000 tons and damaging another 4, for 29,000 tons. Her sixth war mission ended on March 16, 1943, the date when enemy war records reflect that she was probably sunk by enemy action along the equator in the area of the Solomon Islands. Official U.S. Navy records list her as lost as of April 10, 1943. The *Tambor*-class submarine had compiled an impressive record in only 16 months of wartime service.

When the Japanese struck Pearl Harbor, *Triton* was engaged in a practice war patrol off Wake Island. It was not until the night of December 8, when she surfaced to charge batteries, that she learned by radio of the bombing of Pearl Harbor and Wake Island. Before she returned to Pearl Harbor, she fired her four stern torpedoes at a Japanese destroyer from a depth of 120 feet. There was one explosion, but no results were observed, nor did enemy war records later reveal that the torpedoes struck the target.

(text continued on page 201)

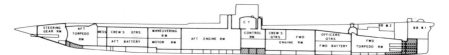

Bass *before (above), and after (below) her conversion into a cargo carrier. The areas converted into cargo space are highlighted in yellow. Other new features include the cut-down conning tower and a peculiar "cigarette deck" aft of the conning tower. The red vertical line forward of the conning tower shows where she broke in half when she struck bottom. The diagram, before the highlighting was added, was taken from* The Fleet Submarine in the U.S. Navy *by Commander John D. Alden, USN (Ret.). Copyright 1979, U.S. Naval Institute; printed by permission.*

A diver preparing to enter the oval hatch in Bass' *conning tower. The chain of the dive-charter boat's grappling hook is wrapped around the pedestal for the 20-mm anti-aircraft guns.* (Photo by Brad Sheard.) ▶

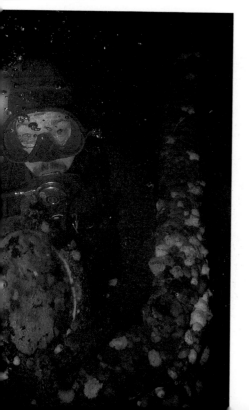

◀ *A diver displays a porthole he recovered from inside* Bass' *conning tower.* (Photo courtesy of Michael deCamp.)

Divers removed seven portholes from Bass' anemone-covered conning tower. A diver looks through one of the empty ports into the submarine's interior. (Photo by H. Keatts.)

Inside Bass' conning tower. (Photo by H. Keatts.)

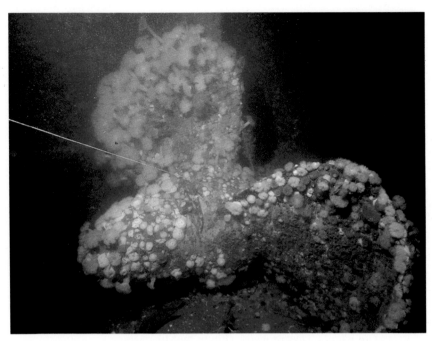

Surprise! Bass' *two manganese bronze, three-bladed, eight-foot diameter screw-propellers have not been removed by salvors yet.* (Photo by Brad Sheard.)

Bass' *aft torpedo room was converted to cargo space. The hatch has not been opened.* (Photo by Brad Sheard.)

Blenny's hull number shows up in sharp contrast, as she lies off Ocean City, Maryland, in about 70 feet of water. (Photo by Mike Moore.)

A diver peers into an open hatch on Bass' *deck.* (Photo by H. Keatts.)

The unusual shark-nosed bow of the Bass *seems ready to swallow this diver.* (Photo by H. Keatts.)

A large tiger shark, surrounded by a school of bait fish, skims over Tarpon's *hull. The bait fish are in no danger. They provide a hiding place for the shark that is lurking in wait for larger prey.* (Photo by Brian Skerry.)

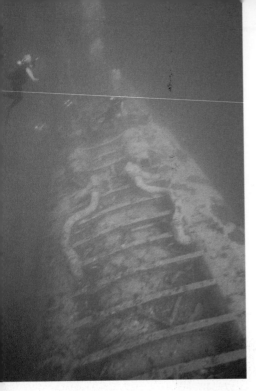

The pressure hull of Tarpon *dwarfs divers as they descend to its deck.* (Photo by H. Keatts.)

Inside Tarpon's *conning tower. Two telegraphs, top and bottom, are visible. Most gauges and instruments have since been removed by divers.* (Photo by Jon Hulburt.)

Open hatches allow divers to penetrate Tarpon's *interior.* (Photo by Brian Skerry.)

Deck support beams provide a skeletal outline behind one of Tarpon's *open hatches.* (Photo by Jon Hulburt.) ▶

▲

Several of Tarpon's *hatches have a five-foot sleeve extending into the interior, which the diver must slide through to penetrate the compartment.* (Photo by Brian Skerry.)

▼ *Author Hank Keatts examines* Tarpon's *four forward torpedo tube doors.* (Photo by Brian Skerry.)

A diver videotapes another diver entering one of Tarpon's hatches. With a set of double tanks on the diver's back, it is a tight fit. (Photo by Brian Skerry.) ▼

▲ This hatch cover has been tied in an open position, so that it will not close accidentally while a diver is inside Tarpon's hull. (Photo by Brian Skerry.)

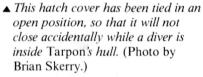

Hovering over Tarpon's pressure hull, a diver checks his bottom time before surfacing. (Photo by H. Keatts.)

(text continued from page 192)

When *Triton* returned to Pearl Harbor, her commanding officer, Lieutenant Commander Willard Ashford Lent, was criticized for not being more aggressive in his encounter with the enemy destroyer. His pre-war training had been to play it safe in such instances, with a sonar attack while submerged. The aggressive successes of German U-boats in the Atlantic with night-time surface attacks had changed the thinking of U.S. naval leaders. That first patrol was the only one of *Triton*'s six that did not produce two or more sinkings. On her third patrol, in the East China Sea, she sank seven ships, one of which was *I-64,* a Japanese submarine.

On February 16, 1943 *Triton* began her last mission, to attack enemy shipping between the Shortland Basin and Rabaul. She attacked a convoy of five destroyer-escorted ships and sank the cargo ship *Kiriha Maru.* Another freighter was damaged. During the attack, one of her torpedoes circled back on the submarine, forcing her to crash dive to evade it. On March 8, another convoy was attacked with eight torpedoes. *Triton* claimed that five of the eight hit, but gunfire from the escorts forced her down before the results could be observed.

The last communication from *Triton* was a message on March 11 that she was chasing two convoys, each of five or more ships. She was informed that *Trigger* (SS-*237*) was operating in an adjacent area, and to restrict her operations south of the Equator. On March 15, *Trigger* reported that she could hear distant depth charges for about an hour after she herself had survived such an attack. That may have been a three-destroyer attack on a submarine slightly northwest of *Triton*'s assigned position. It produced an

The last message received from Triton *stated, "Two groups of smokes, five or more ships each, plus escorts. . . Am chasing." Two days later the submarine was sunk by enemy destroyers.* (Photo courtesy of the Submarine Force Library and Museum.)

oil slick, debris, and items with American identification that may have marked the sinking of *Triton*. *Trigger* was to follow in similar circumstances, two years later.

Trout (SS-*202*)

When the Japanese struck Pearl Harbor, *Trout* was on defensive patrol off Midway Island. She picked up news of the attack early that morning, and was ordered to contact *Argonaut* (SS-*166*), also on patrol but submerged at the time, and give her the news. *Argonaut* was subsequently lost on January 10, 1943 in a surface attack by enemy forces after she was forced to surface by damage from depth charges. *Trout* would follow her 15 months later.

Sources differ regarding the number of enemy ships sunk and damaged by *Trout* in her 11 missions. Japanese war records provide some help, but they are notoriously incomplete and inaccurate. The *Tambor*-class submarine more than accounted for her presence in the war. She has been credited with sinking as many as 24 ships and damaging 7 others. A more conservative estimate would be 16 sunk and 9 damaged—still an impressive record.

As though her combatant record was not enough, *Trout* delivered 3,500 rounds of ammunition to besieged American forces on Corregidor, refueled, and added unusual ballast to compensate for her delivered cargo. Twenty tons of gold bars and silver pesos were loaded aboard for evacuation from the Philippines. Mail and securities were also taken aboard.

Instead of heading back to Pearl Harbor with her valuable cargo, *Trout* continued on to the East China Sea, where she sank the enemy freighter *Chuwa Maru* and a 200-ton patrol ship. Then she ended her second war patrol by returning to Pearl Harbor, where she transferred her valuable cargo to a cruiser for safer keeping.

Lieutenant Commander Albert H. Clark was in command of *Trout* on her eleventh, and final war patrol. Her mission was to patrol the East China Sea again. Japanese war records indicate that a submarine attacked one of their convoys on February 29, 1944 in *Trout*'s assigned area. A large passenger-cargo ship was damaged, and the 7,126-ton transport *Sakito Maru* was sunk. It is possible that *Trout* was sunk by one of the convoy escorts. There is a reference in Japanese war records to an inconclusive antisubmarine attack in her area. But that is only one of several possibilities. Her disappearance is still unsolved.

Trout was declared missing, and presumed lost with her 81-man crew, on April 17, 1944. She was awarded 11 battle stars for World War II service, and three Presidential Unit Citations for her second, third and fifth patrols.

Tullibee *was destroyed as a result of a circular run of one of her torpedoes. Only one crewman, from a total of 80 officers and enlisted men, survived the self-inflicted disaster.* (Photo courtesy of the Submarine Force Library and Museum.)

Tullibee (SS-284)

A single survivor is credited with the only explanation of *Tullibee's* sinking. The *Gato*-class submarine was scheduled to support carrier strikes against Japanese strongholds in the Palaus on March 30-31, 1944. She arrived on station on March 25, and made radar contact with an enemy convoy of a large passenger-cargo ship and two medium sized freighters, accompanied by three escorts. *Tullibee* closed to 3,000 yards and fired two bow torpedoes at the transport. Two minutes later, the submarine was rocked by a violent explosion. One of her torpedoes had run a circular course, back to where it had been fired.

Gunner's Mate Clifford W. Kuykendall was on the bridge when the errant torpedo struck the submarine. He was knocked unconscious by the blast, and thrown into the sea. For ten minutes after he regained consciousness, he heard shouts around him. Other than that, he never heard or saw any other members of the crew. *Tullibee* had disappeared. Enemy hands recovered him from the water, but not before they fired at him with machine guns, weapons that may have disposed of the voices he had heard earlier.

Kuykendall was subjected to interrogation before being transferred to Ofuna Naval Interrogation Camp for more questioning. He remained there six months, then worked in the copper mines at Ashio till the end of the war. Until his repatriation, *Tullibee's* loss was an unsolved mystery to the U.S. Navy.

On her prior three patrols, *Tullibee* had served in the western Caroline Islands, south of Formosa off the China coast, and the Marianas area, sinking three ships (15,500 tons) and damaging three others (22,000 tons). She received three battle stars for World War II service.

Wahoo (SS-238)

The *Gato*-class submarine *Wahoo* survived only 17 months after her May 15, 1942 commissioning, but became one of the most renowned U.S. submarines of World War II. It was not until August 21, that she got underway from Pearl Harbor for her first war patrol, with Lieutenant Commander Marvin G. Kennedy in command. Although three sinkings were claimed on her first two patrols, postwar analysis of Japanese war records credited her with only one.

On December 31, 1942 command of the submarine transferred to her executive officer, Lieutenant Commander Dudley W. Morton, who had earlier commanded *R-4* (SS-*81*) in the Battle of the Atlantic. He had demonstrated both aggressiveness and skill that would earn him the plaudits of his peers, his superiors, the media, and the American public. His performance on *Wahoo's* fourth patrol elicited the terse comment from Pearl Harbor that the, ". . . Japanese think a submarine wolf pack is operating in the Yellow Sea. All shipping tied up."

"Mush" Morton had the friendly nickname bestowed on him by classmates at Annapolis because of his loquacious pastime of telling stories. When he took over command of *Wahoo,* he lost no time letting his crew know exactly what was expected of each man. He announced, *"Wahoo* is expendable. We will take every reasonable precaution, but our mission is to sink enemy shipping. . . Now if anyone doesn't want to go along under these conditions, just see the yeoman. I'm giving him verbal authority to transfer anyone who is not a volunteer. . . Nothing will ever be said about your remaining in Brisbane." No one requested transfer; every member of the crew elected to share with him in his exploits, glory, and death.

Wahoo suffered, with her sister submarines, from the deficiencies of early World War II torpedoes that ran deep, exploded early or not at all, and at times circled back to threaten the submarine that fired them. Despite those obstacles, she was credited with sinking 27 ships for 119,100 tons. Only her sixth patrol was unproductive. Ten torpedoes had been fired in nine attacks, with no damage to enemy shipping. Frustration fired the crew with the need to redeem themselves as soon as possible.

Going, going, gone! Plunging bow-first to the bottom of the Pacific, a Japanese freighter is seen through Wahoo's *periscope.* (Photos courtesy of the Submarine Force Library and Museum.)

Wahoo left Midway on September 13, headed for Japanese waters. She was to enter the Sea of Japan through Peruse Strait on or about September 20, with *Sawfish* (SS-*276*) to follow several days later. On October 5, the Japanese press announced the loss of the 8,000-ton steamer *Konron Maru* to an American submarine near Tsushima Strait. Three other Japanese ships, totaling about 5,300 tons, were also reported sunk in the same area at about the same time.

Japanese war records refer to an antisubmarine patrol plane attack on a surfaced submarine with three depth charges on October 11, the date *Wahoo* was to exit through La Peruse Strait. *Sawfish* had gone through two days earlier, so the target could only have been *Wahoo*. She was announced overdue December 2, and was stricken from the Navy list on December 6, 1943.

Morton was too wiley a skipper to be caught surfaced, unless his submarine had been so severely damaged that she could not submerge. A mine detonation could have been the cause—the shores of the Japanese coastlines had been saturated with mines to cope with growing shipping losses to American submarines. After *Wahoo* failed to return, war missions into the Sea of Japan were suspended until special mine detecting devices were installed on U.S. submarines.

Wahoo was awarded the Presidential Unit Citation for her third patrol, and six battle stars for World War II service.

CHAPTER 14

Additional U.S. Submarine Losses

Accidental Sinkings

- *Cochino* (SS-*345*) was sunk in 1,000+ feet of water, off northern Norway by a battery explosion in 1949.
- *F-1* (SS-*20*) (ex. *Carp*) collided with *F-3* (SS-*22*) and sank off California on December 17, 1917. Nineteen men were lost. The submarine was found in 1976 four and a half miles west of Bird Rock, between Pacific Beach and La Jolla. Her location is 32° 48′30″ N; between 117° 21′27″ and 117° 21′0″ W,; between the 100- and 200-fathom curves.
- *F-4* (SS-*23*) (ex. *Skate*) foundered off Honolulu, Hawaii in 288 feet of water, in March 1915. Twenty-one men were lost. The submarine was raised in August, but sank as she was being towed into shallower water. A private salvage company is considering raising *F-4*.
- *H-1* (SS-*28*) (ex. *Sea Wolf*) grounded in Magdalena Bay, Mexico. She foundered in 9 fathoms of water during salvage operations on March 12, 1920, and four men were lost.

- *O-9* (SS-*70*) foundered June 20, 1941, 24 miles off Portsmouth, N.H., in 440 feet of water.
- *Scorpion* (SSN-*589*) was lost with her entire crew by unknown causes. She sank 400 miles southwest of the Azores in about 6,500 feet of water in May 1968.
- *Stickleback* (SS-*415*) was rammed and sunk by the U.S. destroyer escort *Silverstein* (DE-*534*) on May 30, 1958 off Honolulu, Hawaii.
- *Thresher* (SSN-*593*) was lost with all hands by flooding in the machinery room. She sank near the Isle Shoals in 8,300 feet of water on April 10, 1963.

U.S. Subs Lost After Transfer to Foreign Countries

- *Blower* (SS-*325*) was transferred to Turkey in 1950. In 1953, she was rammed and sunk in the Dardenelles by the Swedish freighter *Naboland*.
- *Catfish* (SS-*339*) was transferred to Argentina in 1971 and renamed *Santa Fe* (S-*21*). During the 1982 Falkland War, she was caught alongside a pier and was machine gunned by British aircraft. She was beached in a bay on South Georgia Island; her present status is unknown.
- *Diablo* (SS-*479*) was transferred to Pakistan in 1964. She was sunk in the Bay of Bengal by an internal mine explosion in 1971 during the war with India.
- *R-3* (SS-*80*) was loaned to Britain early in World War II and renamed *P-511*. She was "lost as a result of perils of the sea" on November 21, 1947. There were no survivors.
- *R-19* (SS-*96*) was loaned to Britain in 1942 and renamed *P-514*. She was rammed in the West Atlantic by H.M.C.S. *Georgian* on June 21, 1942. She sank with no survivors.
- *S-29* (SS-*134*) was loaned to Britain in 1944 and redesignated *P-556*. She ran aground at Portsmouth, England. In 1986, her hull was cut up and shipped to Spain for scrap.

U.S. Submarines Sunk as Targets or Hulks

- Six submarines, *A-2* (SS-*3*), (ex. *Adder*), *A-3* (SS-*4*) (ex. *Grampus*), *A-4* (SS-*5*) (ex. *Moccasin*), *A-5* (SS-*6*) (ex. *Pike*), *A-6* (SS-*7*) (ex. *Porpoise*), and *A-7* (SS-*8*) (ex. *Shark*) were sunk as targets off the Chesapeake Capes in the early 1920s.
- *Apogon* (SS-*308*), see Bikini Atoll.
- *Aspro* (SS-*309*), was torpedoed by *Pomodon* (SS-*486*) off San Diego, California on November 16, 1962.

- *B-1* (SS-*10*), (ex. *Viper*), *B-2* (SS-*11*) (ex. *Cuttlefish*), and *B-3* (SS-*12*) (ex. *Tarantula*) were sunk as targets in Manila Bay, Philippines. *B-2* was sunk in 1919, *B-1* and *B-3* in 1921.
- *Balao*'s (SS-*285*) conning tower was removed and she was sunk as a target off Charleston, S.C. (30° 46'5"N, 74° 11'W) on September 4, 1963.
- *Barbero* (SS-*317*) was torpedoed off Pearl Harbor, Hawaii by *Greenfish* (SS-*351*) on October 7, 1964.
- Bikini Atoll. The U.S. Navy gathered an array of over ninety ships at Bikini Atoll in July 1946, to determine the effects of 20- and 50-kiloton atomic bombs. The target fleet included U.S. Navy, Japanese, and German vessels. It would have comprised the world's fifth largest navy at the time, including aircraft carriers, battleships, and even submarines.

   Two new U.S. submarines, *Dentuda* (SS-*335*) and *Parche* (SS-*384*), survived the detonations of two atomic bombs and saw service again. Four, *Searaven* (SS-*196*), *Skate* (SS-*305*), *Skipjack* (SS-*184*), and *Tuna* (SS-*203*) were raised and sunk by aircraft off California in 1948. *Pilotfish* (SS-*386*) was raised and sunk as a target off Eniwetok in October 1948. One U.S. submarine, *Apogon* (SS-*308*), remains in the shallow waters of Bikini Atoll. Scuba divers have been exploring some of Bikini's wrecks since the 1970s.
- *Blackfin* (SS-*322*), was designated as a target in 1978. Her present status and location are unknown.
- *Bluegill* (SS-*242*) was awarded four battle stars for World War II service. She also received the Navy Unit Commendation for her first war patrol during which she sank three Japanese vessels, including the light cruiser *Yubari*.

   On December 3, 1970, the *Gato*-class submarine was sunk in 125 feet of water off Lahaina, Maui, Hawaii as a U.S. Navy salvage training hulk. Sport divers, however, were using the site and the Navy was concerned about residual liability. A Navy salvage crew from *Brunswick*

Bluegill (SS-242) after being raised from 125 feet of water by U.S. Navy divers. (Composite photo by Tim Keatts.)

(ATS-*3*) raised the submarine in November 1983. She was scuttled in over 1,000 feet of water as a deterrent to sport divers.

- *Bream* (SS-*243*) was torpedoed by *Sculpin* (SSN-*590*) off Point Arguello, California on November 8, 1969.
- *Bugara* (SS-*331*) was designated a target, but foundered off Cape Flattery, Washington on June 1, 1971 while being towed to the target area.
- *Burrfish* (SS-*312*) was sunk off San Clemente, California, on November 19, 1969.
- *Carbonero* (SS-*337*) was sunk as a weapons target by *Pogy* (SSN-*647*) off Pearl Harbor, Hawaii on April 27, 1975.
- *Chopper* (SS-*342*) was used as a salvage and rescue hulk from 1971 to 1976. She foundered off Florida in 2,400 fathoms on July 21, 1976 while being rigged as a tethered underwater target.
- *Dentuda* (SS-*335*) see Bikini Atoll.
- *Devilfish* (SS-*292*) was torpedoed by *Wahoo* (SS-*565*) off San Francisco, California on October 19, 1968.
- *Guardfish* (SS-*217*) was sunk as a torpedo target by *Devilfish* (SS-*350*) and *Blenny* (SS-*324*), 97 miles south of Block Island.
- *Guavina* (SS-*362*) was torpedoed by *Cubera* (SS-*347*) off Cape Henry on November 14, 1967.
- *Jack* (SS-*259*) was transferred to Greece in April 1958. She was returned to U.S. ownership in 1967, to be sunk in the Mediterranean as a target by the Sixth Fleet on September 5, 1967.
- *Manta* (SS-*299*) was sunk by aircraft off Norfolk, Virginia on July 16, 1969.
- *Menhaden* (SS-*377*) was struck from the Navy list in 1973 and used as a tethered underwater target off Keyport, Washington. Her present status is unknown.
- *Moray* (SS-*300*) was torpedoed and sunk off San Clemente, California on June 18, 1970.
- *Muskallunge* (SS-*262*) earned five battle stars during World War II. The submarine was transferred to Brazil in 1957 and renamed *Humaita*. She was returned to the U.S. Navy ten years later and sunk off Narragansett Bay as a target by *Tench* (SS-*417*) on July 9, 1968.
- *O-12* (SS-*73*) was scuttled on November 20, 1931 in a Norwegian fjord in 350 meters of water.
- *Parche* (SS-*384*), see Bikini Atoll.
- *Pilotfish* (SS-*386*), see Bikini Atoll.
- *Queenfish* (SS-*393*) was torpedoed by *Swordfish* (SSN-*579*) on August 14, 1963.

- *Redfish* (SS-*395*) was torpedoed by *Sea Fox* (SS-*402*) off San Diego, California, on February 6, 1969.
- *S-4* (SS-*109*) was rammed by the Coast Guard cutter *Paulding* off Cape Cod in December 1927. Forty officers and men died in the tragedy. Three months later the submarine was raised and repaired. She served for another eight years before she was scuttled off Hawaii in May 1936.
- *Sabalo* (SS-*302*) was sunk as a target off San Diego, California in 1973.
- *Sea Devil* (SS-*400*) was torpedoed by elements of Submarine Flotilla 12 off southern California on November 24, 1964.
- *Sealion* (SS-*315*) was sunk in 1978 as a target off Long Island, at 39° 04′ N, 70° 12′ W.
- *Searaven* (SS-*196*), see Bikini Atoll.
- *Segundo* (SS-*398*) was sunk by *Salmon* (SS-*573*) with a MK 37 torpedo on August 8, 1970.
- *Skate* (SS-*305*), see Bikini Atoll.
- *Skipjack* (SS-*184*), see Bikini Atoll.
- *Sterlet* (SS-*392*) was sunk by *Sargo* (SSN-*583*) as a torpedo target on January 31, 1969, off Hawaii, in 8,000 feet of water.
- *Tigrone* (SS-*419*) was sunk as a target, on October 25, 1976, off Cape Hatteras at 36° 09′2″ N, 71° 15′3″ W.
- *Tinosa* (SS-*283*) was scuttled in November 1960 as an antisubmarine warfare weapons and sonar target.
- *Tiru* (SS-*416*) was rigged as a remote control target and sunk off the Virginia Capes (36° 05′3″ N, 71° 15′3″ W) in 1979 by *Silversides* (SSN-*679*), in an MK 38 torpedo test.
- *Trepang* (SS-*412*) was sunk on September 16, 1969 by gunfire from the U.S. destroyers *Henderson* (DD-*785*) and *Fechteler* (DD-*870*), off southern California.
- *Tuna* (SS-*203*), see Bikini Atoll.
- *Tunny* (SS-*282*) was torpedoed by *Volador* (SS-*490*) on June 19, 1970.

BIBLIOGRAPHY

Alden, Commander John D. *The Fleet Submarine in the U.S. Navy.* Naval Institute Press, 1985.

"Another Try at Raising Sunken Sub *G-2* Progressing; Two Trys Failed." *Norwich Bulletin,* August 31, 1957.

The "Argonaut:" Her Evolution and History. The Lake Submarine Co., 1900.

Bachand, Robert G. *Scuba Northeast, Volume II.* Sea Sports Publications, 1986.

Bagnasco, Erminio. *Submarines of World War Two.* Naval Institute Press, 1977.

Barnes, Robert H. *U.S. Submarines.* H.F. Morse Associated, Inc., 1944.

Bishop, Farnham. *The Story of the Submarine.* Century Company, 1942.

Blair, Jr., Clay. *Silent Victory.* J.B. Lippincott Co., 1975.

"*Blenny* Sub Becomes New Maryland Artificial Reef." *Underwater USA,* August 1989.

Bolander, Louis H. "The *Alligator,* First Federal Submarine of the Civil War." *U.S. Naval Institute Proceedings,* 1938.

"Brave Old Sub Tarpon Escapes Scrap Pile for a Watery Atlantic Grave." *New London Day,* August 27, 1957.

Burgess, Robert F. *Ships Beneath the Sea: A History of Subs and Submersibles.* McGraw-Hill Book Co., 1975.

Cahill, Bob. "New England's Saga of Sunken Subs." *Skin Diver,* September 1964.

Cahill, Robert E. and Tzimoulis, Paul. "Realm of Sunken Adventure: Depth-charged *G-2* of World War I Attracts Sport Divers All Along Eastern Seaboard." *The Courant Magazine,* June 25, 1961.

Cardone, Bonnie J. and Smith, Patrick. *Shipwrecks of Southern California.* Menasha Ridge Press, 1989.

Chambliss, William C. *The Silent Service.* Signet Books, 1959.

Churchill, Winston. *The Second World War.* Houghton Mifflin, 1948-53.

Davis, Burke. *The Civil War: Strange & Fascinating Facts.* The Fairfax Press, 1982.

Davitt, Stephen. "Ocean City To Get Navy Sub For Reef." *Underwater USA,* January 1988.

Dictionary of American Naval Fighting Ships. Naval History Division, Office of the Chief of Naval Operations, 1969.

"The Disaster to One of Our Latest Submarines." *Scientific American,* September 25, 1920.

Farb, Roderick M. *Shipwrecks: Diving the Graveyard of the Atlantic.* Menasha Ridge Press, 1985.

Farb, Roderick M. "The *Tarpon.*" *Skin Diver,* March 1985.

Farb, Roderick M. "USS *Blenny.*" *Skin Diver,* December 1989.

Field, Cyril. *The Story of the Submarine.* Simpson, Low, Marston & Co., 1908.

"Finally: Sub *G-2* Blown Apart." *New London Day,* July 2, 1962.

Gable, Frank T. *The Birth and Development of the American Submarine.* Harper & Bros., 1924.

Gentile, Gary. *Shipwrecks of New Jersey.* Sea Sports Publications, 1988.

Gentile, Gary. "Chance Discovery." *Scubapro Diving and Snorkeling,* Winter 1987.

Gentile, Gary. "Blackwater Sub." *Scubapro Diving and Snorkeling,* Spring 1988.

Hoehling, A.A. *The Great War at Sea: A History of Naval Action 1914-18.* Galahad Books, 1965.

Holmes, W.J. *Undersea Victory.* Doubleday & Co., 1966.

Hoyt, Edwin P. *Submarines at War: the history of the American silent service.* Stein & Day, 1983.

"Hulk Off Block Island Thought Submarine Bass." *New London Day,* July 19, 1966.

Keatts, Henry. *New England's Legacy of Shipwrecks.* American Merchant Marine Museum Press, 1988.

Kimball, Carol W. "Decoy." *Sea Classics,* November 1974.

Kolintz, Harry Von. "The Confederate Submarine." *U.S. Naval Institute Proceedings,* October 1937.

"L-8 Launched 35 Years Ago." *Portsmouth Periscope,* May 2, 1952.

Land, E.S. *Early History of Submarines.* U.S. Government Printing Office, 1916.

Leckie, Robert. *The Wars of America.* Harper & Row, Publishers, 1981.

Lenton, H.T. *American Submarines.* Doubleday, 1973.

Lipscomb, F.W. *Historic Submarines.* Praeger Publishers, 1970.

Lockwood, Charles A. *Down to the Sea in Subs.* W.W. Norton & Co., 1967.

McCombs, Don and Worth, Fred L. *World War II Super Facts.* Warner Books, 1983.

Moale, Dick. "The Tragic Loss of USS *S-5* off Cape May, New Jersey." *Atlantic Coastal Diver,* April 1980.

Morison, Samuel Eliot. *History of the United States Naval Operations in World War II.* Little, Brown & Company, 1956.

Morris, Richard K. *John P. Holland.* Naval Institute Press, 1966.

Morrison, Gary R., and Bishop, David J. *United States Submarine Data Book.* Submarine Force Library & Museum Assoc., Inc., 1984.

Naval History Division. *Dictionary of American Naval Fighting Ships.* Office of the Chief of Naval Operations, 1969.

Naval History Division. *United States Submarine Losses – World War II.* Office of the Chief of Naval Operations, 1963.

Polmar, Norman. *The American Submarine.* The Nautical & Aviation Publishing Co. of America, 1983.

Pike, William P. "Sea Devils Dive to Sub Sunk in 1919." *The Hartford Times,* August 12, 1957.

Pratt, Fletcher. *The Compact History of the United States Navy.* Hawthron Books, Inc., 1967.

"Rescuing the Crew Imprisoned Hours in Submarine *S-5.*" *New York Times,* September 3, 1920.

Roach, Thomas. "The Secret of the USS *Bass.*" *Skin Diver,* October 1977.

Roland, Alex. *Underwater Warfare in the Age of Sail.* Indiana University Press, 1978.

Roscoe, Theodore. *Pig Boats.* Bantam Books, 1949.

Roscoe, Theodore. *United States Submarine Operations In World War II.* United States Naval Institute, 1949.

Rowbotham, W.B. "Robert Fulton's Turtle Boat." *U.S. Naval Institute Proceedings,* December 1936.

Sanders, Harry. "The First American Sub." *U.S. Naval Institute Proceedings,* December 1936.

Speck, Robert M. "The Connecticut Water Machine Versus the Royal Navy." *American Heritage,* December 1980.

Stover, Rusti. "The Little Pigs That Went To War." *Sea Classics,* April/May 1985.

"The Submarine With Notes On Care and Operations." Compiled by The Department of Submarines and Torpedoes, Submarine School, New London, 1920.

"Sub Sunk Off Block Island?" *Norwich Bulletin,* February 16, 1966.

"Sunken Sub off Block Island Is Identified." *Norwich Bulletin,* July 19, 1966.

Sweetman, Jack. *American Naval History.* Naval Institute Press, 1984.

Traver, Judith. "Local Men Dive to Sunken Submarine." *West Hartford News,* August 8, 1957.

Whitehouse, Arthur George Joseph. *Subs and Submariners.* Doubleday, 1961.

"Wigwagging Shirt Brings Rescuers to Entombed Crew." *New York Times,* September 4, 1920.

Yarmin, Ray de. "The Rescue of the S-5." *Anchor News,* July/August 1980.

INDEX

215

Let these Pisces Diving and Snorkeling Guides show you the underwater wonders of —

Australia
Bahamas: Nassau and
  New Providence Island
Belize
Bonaire
California
Channel Islands
Cozumel
Dive into History:
  U-Boats
  U.S. Submarines
  Warships
Family Islands and
  Grand Bahamas
Florida Keys and East Coast
Cayman Islands

Great Lakes
Hawaii
The Joy of Snorkeling
Shipwreck Diving:
  North Carolina
  Southern California
Texas
Treasure Hunting with a
  Metal Detector
Treasure of the Atocha
Undersea Predators
The Underwater Dig —
  An Introduction to Marine
  Archaeology
Virgin Islands, U.S. and British